A Plea
for a Social
and Ecological
Urbanism

Maarten Hajer
Peter Pelzer
Martijn van den Hurk
Chris ten Dam
Edwin Buitelaar

Neighbourhoods for the Future

trancity×valiz

Contents

Preface

This book is based on the conviction that the climate crisis requires us to broaden our 'urban imagination'. The need to re-imagine our urban future is particularly astute as we have built cities based on the easy availability and unproblematic use of coal, oil, and gas over the last 150 years. Cities have grown as the automobile allowed us to live further away from work. We have changed our personal ideas of the good life accordingly. For a long time, the best many people could hope for was the 'American dream' of a family home, with a green lawn and a car in the driveway, somewhere quiet and safe in the suburbs. But this lifestyle now proves to be a cul-de-sac itself. Similarly, the architect's dream of living in towers in the park has not been delivered. These modernist ideas were also intertwined with the fossil age, autmotive technology, and the prevalence of private mobility. Yet currently, science shows we cannot square this type of urban life with completing the transition to a sustainable world, one that keeps the increase in global warming well below 2 degrees, preferably below 1.5 degrees. That is why we now need new 'imaginaries' of urban life, and preferably ones that persuasively show that life in a post-fossil city can be considerably better in terms of living standards than the urban lifestyles we aspired to in the twentieth century.

In this book we put forward the neighbourhood as a very potent alternative. Cities have always had neighbourhoods, of course, but now they take on a new significance as an urban form that allows us to combine fighting the global sustainability crisis with the wish to improve our general quality of life. While many would regard neighbourhoods as an anachronistic debate, we see them as the next step in the debate on urbanism. In this book we understand urbanism as efforts to understand patterns of urbanization in combination with the wish to help create thriving cities.

Our plea for a social and ecological urbanism aims to correct the tendency to think about urban futures primarily at larger levels of scale. Looking at the current discourse we see a lot of attention for global statistics. While we have no reason to question the UN DESA statistics that suggest that in 2050 66 percent of the global population will live in cities, we also see the limitations of this approach. We live in an urban age in which urbanization is a planetary phenomenon.[1] But how can we act upon this challenge? How can we maximize our efforts to make sure that those active in making planning decisions are inspired and enabled to create better places for people to live in? This book offers neighbourhoods for the future as a 'modest imaginary'; not as a prescription, but as a point of orientation.

Neighbourhoods are spatial units that people can relate to, writes Emily Talen in one of the rare new books on the topic of neighbourhoods.[2]

[1] R. Burdett and P. Rode, eds., *Shaping Cities in an Urban Age* (London: Phaidon Press, 2018); N. Brenner, ed., *Implosions/ Explosions: Towards a Study of Planetary Urbanization* (Berlin: Jovis, 2014).

[2] E. Talen, *Neighborhood* (Oxford: Oxford University Press, 2019).

Yet the idea of a 'generic' city seems to prevail over studying what makes for good neighbourhoods. Interestingly, if we go back in the literature of urban studies we find a rich resource of thinking about what makes for good neighbourhoods—a resource that we could draw on again, today. In this book we place the neighbourhood centre stage, analyzing the sustainable futures we may build with the neighbourhood as building block. Our social and ecological urbanism is based on a re-appreciation of what is characteristic of well-functioning neighbourhoods. In this sense this book is firmly rooted in an urban studies perspective. However, we warn that a social and ecological turn in urbanism requires getting rid of many commitments and inclinations of its twentieth-century predecessors: the idea of the expert-urbanist who comes up with generally applicable solutions; the idea that the urgency of policy issues requires speed rather than care; the idea that the know-how of 'street-level bureaucrats' would not be relevant in making neighbourhoods a success.

We wanted to write a book that does not only help to *understand* what sustainable neighbourhoods are and how to get there, but that also actually contributes to *shaping* these neighbourhoods. 'Future forming', as the psychologist and philosopher Kenneth Gergen calls this type of research.[3] We hope that the reader will be inspired, puzzled, or energized to research, contribute to, or reflect on neighbourhoods for the future.

Then COVID-19 struck. We had completed the manuscript of this book, were putting in the final corrections to the text, and were searching for photos when, all of a sudden, the world seemed to come to a near standstill. Images circulated of empty streets and unoccupied subways, of people wearing masks, of guards policing 'social distancing', potentially undermining the message of this book. Yet while it is clear that the pandemic will deeply affect our urban futures, we think this book also speaks to the choice we can make, indeed have to make, in the near future. After all, we also saw pictures of people taking back the street to play, we heard of plans to now radically create more space for pedestrians and bicycles while pushing out the car, in cities like Paris, Vienna, London, or New York. Indeed, we think the pandemic puts on the table the need to really actively think about the future of our cities. And in this context our argument for a social and ecological urbanism with a pivotal role for well-functioning neighbourhood can, hopefully, play a role. The neighbourhood, as the scale between the home and the city, has the promise to give city life its room to breathe, add to its resilience and its social capacity to cope with the unexpected.

About This Book

This book contains four parts. In the <u>first part</u> → p. 13 we reflect on what the climate crisis means for cities, drawing on major studies written on the topic. Based on that, we lay out our idea of the neighbourhood as a crucial level in the coming decades of urbanization.

[3] K.J. Gergen, 'From Mirroring to World-making: Research as Future Forming', *Journal for the Theory of Social Behaviour* 45, no. 3 (2015), pp. 287–310.

We also develop our notion of a social and ecological urbanism and coin two theoretical concepts: 'neighbourhood ecology' and 'neighbourhood arrangement'. The former allows to make an inventory of crucial *qualities* of a neighbourhood, the latter allows for an *analysis* of why certain neighbourhoods could develop these qualities. In that sense they assist the efforts to create high-quality neighbourhoods elsewhere. Our plea for an 'ecological turn' in urbanism aspires to reconnect the often somewhat technological and physical agendas of the sustainability sciences to the social knowledge about what makes vibrant neighbourhoods.

The second part → p. 41 of the book consists of 'vignettes' of existing 'neighbourhoods for the future' initiatives—some completed, others under construction or envisioned. Our experience is that there is a huge appetite for good examples. We made an inventory of over a hundred 'neighbourhoods for the future', characterized by high sustainability ambitions. We present thirteen of these neighbourhoods as 'vignettes'. In these vignettes we describe some key characteristics of the neighbourhoods and try and highlight their particular qualities. They are all remarkable and inspiring in their own way. Some show the possibility of truly radical choices in bringing down energy consumption (Hunziker Areal, Zurich → p. 64), while others highlight the need to have a critical debate on what role 'smart' technology should play in future neighbourhoods (Villiers Island, Toronto → p. 110, and Kalasatama, Helsinki → p. 70). Some show how durable some neighbourhoods are that were designed according to ecological principles (GWL, Amsterdam → p. 58), others show how to connect the goals of the circular economy to planning new neighbourhoods (BedZED, London → p. 48). Together these vignettes give us a good sense of what we can see as cutting-edge approaches to making neighbourhoods more sustainable. None of them are entirely perfect, yet all possess promising elements that other neighbourhoods may want to learn from.

The third part → p. 117 of the book consists of three in-depth case studies. We studied Bo01 in Malmö, Sweden, Regent Park in Toronto, Canada, and Overvecht in Utrecht, the Netherlands. We do not consider these cases as 'best practices', but have singled them out because they can teach us much about the effort to create neighbourhoods for the future.

Bo01 → p. 122 is one of the best-known cases of the early wave of 'sustainable neighbourhoods' of the 1990s and 2000s. Located in a former shipyard district in Malmö, in the very south of Sweden, it was meant to be a showcase of a new style of living. Bo01 was to mark the transition of Malmö from an industrial harbour town, with shipyards and manufacturing industries, to a service economy—with Calatrava's 'Turning Torso' as a central eyecatcher. We revisited the neighbourhood to see what worked and what did not quite work, how this can be explained, and what we can learn from Bo01.

Regent Park → p. 148 is a case of a remarkable transformation of an old modernist development into a thriving neighbourhood in Toronto, Canada. Heralded as a neighbourhood of the future in the 1940s and early 1950s, Regent Park was built following the modernist design rules of the likes of Le Corbusier, eradicating the old street pattern, building superblocks and 'towers in the park'. The transformation of this modernist neighbourhood, which started in 2006, resulted in a place with a markedly different social makeup and higher density, and with so many amenities that the neighbourhood, once notorious for crime and drugs, now receives visitors from other parts of the city to attend the local film festival, play cricket, or work on their professional education. Sustainable standards were followed as a matter of course, but due to energy-inefficient behaviour of their residents, buildings holding the highest sustainability certificates do not always perform accordingly. Moreover, there is a trade-off behind the whole redevelopment: the city sold parcels of land to private developers to make the business case work.

Overvecht, Utrecht → p. 178 is the *pars pro toto* for the many neighbourhoods with modernist high-rise that emerged all over the northern hemisphere in the post-war period. It classifies as what Dutch policymakers these days refer to as a 'vulnerable' neighbourhood, with people's lives marked by health problems, unemployment, and crime. Interestingly, and in contrast to Toronto's Regent Park, in Overvecht there is no talk of demolishing the existing high-rise. Here we see a variety of approaches in which different (coalitions of) actors congregate to define and operate projects to improve the quality of the neighbourhood, both in the short and long term. In the meantime, housing associations are busy insulating their housing stock and providing alternatives for natural-gas-based cooking and heating. The case sheds an interesting light on the possibilities for change, on how projects, when seen in interconnection, may together work towards a better neighbourhood.

The fourth part → p. 201 of this book is devoted to our analysis and findings. We have drawn up a set of nine lessons-cum-recommendations, both in terms of the qualities to pursue (i.e. neighbourhood ecologies) and the particular neighbourhood arrangements that can help realize high-quality urban neighbourhoods.

Two caveats. First of all, this is not a cookbook. We do not provide a manual for how to proceed: we do not end with 'decision rules' on how to make well-functioning neighbourhoods. The core of what we investigated in the in-depth case studies was: what happened to those places that once were or are currently being promoted as 'neighbourhoods for the future'? Each of these three cases reveals a nuanced picture; they include things we could perhaps replicate in other cities, but also mistakes we should definitely not repeat. Likewise, each of the vignettes has one or more distinct qualities, yet none of them is an unambiguous utopia. Such neighbourhoods do not exist and that is probably for the better.

Secondly, we are aware that this book has a bias towards the Global North. Our case studies come from Europe, and, to a lesser extent, North America. Our insights mostly apply to these contexts. The irony is clear: many future neighbourhoods will be built in the Global South and we would like to contribute to that discussion. However, given the practical and epistemic limitations, we take a humble stance in this regard. Having said that, we are curious to learn and engage in further discussions and we suggest that some of the concepts we develop may have value for the ultra-dynamic urban contexts of Africa or South Asia, and for those places struggling to dislodge the default of modernist high-rise with its characteristically weak social ecologies.

So, how to read this book? It makes sense to start with the essay and end with the conclusions. Other than that, there is no strict chronological or analytical order in which we present the vignettes and the in-depth cases. One can read them either sequentially or in random order.

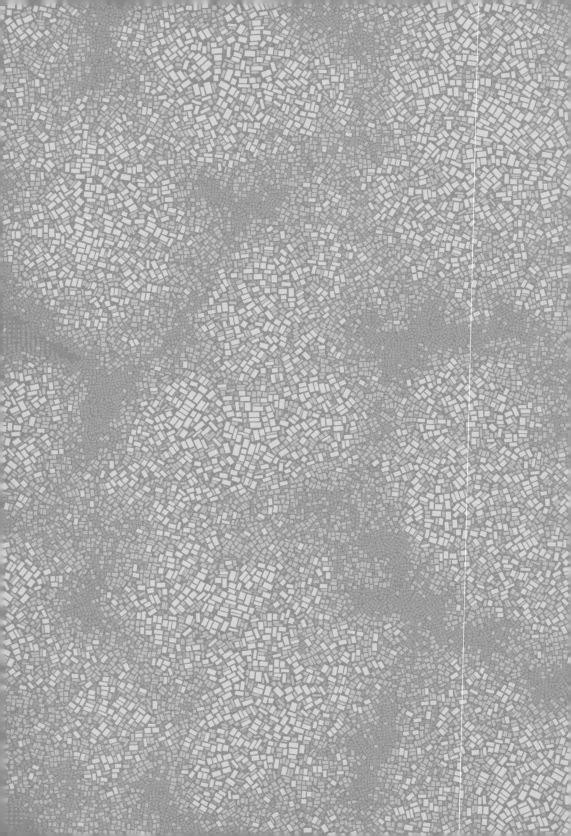

1 (Re)building Cities from the Neighbourhood Up

The Sense of a Neighbourhood

Four people are chatting in front of Quartiersladen → Fig. 1.1, the local shop. It is a rainy day in the neighbourhood of Vauban → p. 104 in Freiburg, Germany, yet they take their time. One of them is holding a bicycle, another carries two bags of groceries. A child pulls at her father's arm to make him move along. 'This is precisely what we had imagined when we developed the neighbourhood. If we would keep cars at a distance, integrate shops in the housing blocks, and create a broad pavement for pedestrians while allowing bicycles, we might create the circumstances for people to meet, for conviviality', says Philipp, a long-time resident.

Vauban is celebrated internationally as a 'green' neighbourhood, scoring high on nearly all sustainability criteria. It is known for its 'passive houses': houses that produce more energy than the households themselves require; for its mobility strategy, privileging bicycles and public transport; and for its soft relationship with the natural environment surrounding it. Yet, standing at the corner of the Kurt-Tucholsky-Straße and the Vauban Allee in Freiburg, and seeing how people socialize, the social qualities of this neighbourhood are arguably at least as remarkable.

Above all, Vauban leaves you with a sense of possibility; the feeling that there are alternatives to how we usually build cities; the awareness that making our cities climate-proof and making them more sociable and pleasant places to live in at the same time, is possible. Shops are locally-owned. Philipp points at a large wood-fired pizza oven that was built in one of the pocket parks in between the housing blocks. It was expensive to construct and the municipality was reluctant to put it in, wary of vandalism and the cost of maintenance. 'It is there for anyone to use. You just pick up the key from that shop over there, unlock it and it is ready for use. We have never had any trouble. On the contrary, people are proud of it and cherish it.'

This book is about neighbourhoods. It is a plea for revisiting what was once a cornerstone of urbanism and now deserves to take centre stage again. We have assigned our cities the grandiose task of becoming 'climate neutral' in 2025, 2030, or 2040. CO_2 reduction is crucial, but how will people *live* in those cities? Can we make cities better places to live in while we are busy reducing our carbon footprint? Can we also connect the leading 'CO_2 agenda' to other issues of environment and health, such as air pollution, contaminated soil, and sustainable resource use in general? Can we make the connection between urbanism and sustainable living, culminating in sustainable ways of life? We think

Fig. 1.1 ↑ Quartiersladen: a shop owned and operated by a collective of Vauban residents who live in the building.

there are many ways to combine sustainability and sociability. For this, neighbourhoods are the crucial point of intervention. We should rebuild our cities from the neighbourhood up and dare to make them better places.

However, if we want to help rebuild our cities with such social qualities in mind, we need to understand what determines that quality, and when and how it actually got built. Throughout this book, we seek to stretch the imagination of what is possible, create a new appetite to make better cities and tap into a new level of ambition. We coin two new concepts. First of all, the notion of *neighbourhood ecologies* to refer to the qualities in which sustainability can be combined with enhanced sociability. Moreover, we seek to reveal why certain neighbourhoods became so successful. We do this by analyzing the particular *neighbourhood arrangements* that help understand why neighbourhoods develop certain characteristics. Applying this to the case of Vauban, you cannot understand the social and physical qualities that they have achieved without appreciating the legal rules that gave the developments rights to *Baugruppen,* small cooperatives of people who wanted to live there. They built the apartment blocks that comprise the neighbourhood. The Baugruppen pooled money and plans and were able to leverage bank loans to actually construct the linear blocks of about fifty units typical for the district. It reminds us that behind remarkable ecological and social qualities there always is a unique neighbourhood arrangement, made up of ideas, actors, rules, and resources. And perhaps it is this particular neighbourhood arrangement that Vauban should be at least as famous for.

Cities in Times of the Climate Crisis

We argue that neighbourhoods are the best entry point for making better cities. But we argue this case knowing that the main challenge for our cities in the coming decades is dealing with the climate crisis. We will have to make sure that our cities, our buildings, our transportation, indeed, our very organization of urban life, is reorganized in such a way as to first stop the rise of CO_2 emissions and then to bring emissions down to about one tenth of the current levels.[1] Moreover, with erratic weather patterns, from heat waves to torrential rains, we will have to make sure we can cope with the disruptions caused by human-caused climate change. We will need cooler and more resilient cities.

If we continue to build cities as we did in the twentieth century, we will simply blow the fuses of the planet, as Mark Swilling once put it. We cannot afford to build cities at very low densities using ever more concrete, steel, and tarmac. We urgently need to change our way of urban development. The established UN DESA statistics suggest that 66 percent of the world's population will be living in cities in 2050.[2] To house all those new residents a stunning 40 percent of the urban fabric of 2050 still has to be built,

[1] IRP, *The Weight of Cities: Resource Requirements of Future Urbanization* (Nairobi: International Resource Panel, United Nations Environment Programme, 2018).

[2] United Nations, Department of Economic and Social Affairs, Population Division, *World Urbanization Prospects: The 2014 Revision* (New York, NY: United Nations, 2015).

Urban Land use (million km²)

Growth in urban land area by region,
2010–2050, if historical trend of
de-densification annum continues.

* Caucasus,
  Central Asia and
  Eastern Europe

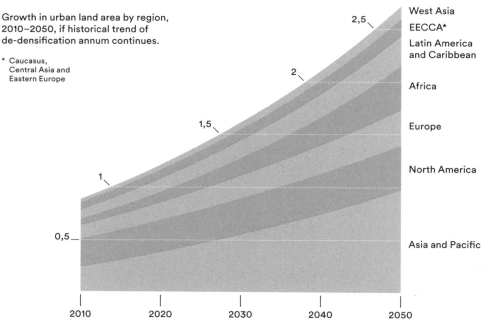

West Asia

EECCA*

Latin America
and Caribbean

Africa

Europe

North America

Asia and Pacific

2,5

2

1,5

1

0,5

2010   2020   2030   2040   2050

Fig. 1.2 ↑ Extrapolation of
the dominant trend of
de-densification – building cities
outward. IRP, *The Weight of Cities*, 2018.

predominantly in Asia and Africa. In a recent study,
The Weight of Cities, a group of academics working for
the UN International Resource Panel (IRP) calculated
the resource requirements for this future urbanization.[3]
The dominant trend is one of de-densification, of building cities out-
wards by 2 percent per year → Fig. 1.2, resulting in an increased reliance
on cars and motorways, locking cities into high consumption of fossil
fuels and other natural resources.

We now have to find a way to alter this trend. This
will have to start with changing our way of thinking about the urban
environment. Using the neighbourhood as our lens, we see a new
sort of cityscape emerging, with much more emphasis on cool, green
space, on water retention, with more human interaction, with public
or shared forms of transport and with all sorts of amenities close-by
so as to avoid having to travel longer distances on a daily basis. Well-
functioning, ecological neighbourhoods taking the place of sprawling
suburbs and dysfunctional high-rise. Of course, such neighbourhoods
do not stand alone, but are functionally, socially, and institutionally
linked to each other and are nested in a wider urban context.

To arrive at this reimagination, we suggest liaising with
the power of the current wave of actions to cut emissions and 'climate
proof' our cities. Housing insulation is high on the
[3] IRP, *The Weight of Cities*, 2018.   agenda, using district heating and electricity to heat

our homes and replace natural gas infrastructures is on the table, and replacing coal-fired power stations with renewable energy sources is well underway. This is a very powerful force, involving hundreds of billions of euros and dollars. Yet we see a real risk that, if left to its own devices, climate policy may become a technology-focused and even technocratic quest that creates little social support on the way. Indeed, and probably much more likely, that it will meet with fierce social opposition resulting in slow implementation. Instead, we argue to approach planetary challenges from the neighbourhood up, directly linking the interventions to local concerns.

The urgency to rethink how we build and transform our cities is broader than climate change. We are now at the beginning of what will be a sustained period of 'climate proofing' our cities. Partly, this will be about dealing with the emerging consequences of the climate crisis, but surely it will also be about getting CO_2 equivalents out of the energy mix, out of our diets, out of our way of moving about. This is a phase of fierce debates about the relative merits of district heating systems, heat pumps, private versus shared mobility, reprioritizing the roads and streets for either CO_2-intense or CO_2-free or -low forms of transport, individual versus collective solutions, certification schemes, or the (relative) potential of geothermal solutions. However, while recognizing the central importance of the climate crisis in urban strategies, it would be a mistake to work towards CO_2 reduction as a single purpose pursuit. Instead, we suggest it makes more sense and will be more effective to try and merge the effort to curb CO_2 and make cities climate-proof (that is, able to deal with heat, drought and torrential rains) with the effort to make them healthier and socially more just. Indeed, we argue that we need to create places that are not only resilient but all-around more pleasant places to live in, places that bring out the best in people. Then the level of the neighbourhood suddenly is crucial in realizing this planetary task.

Why Neighbourhoods?

Kreuzberg in Berlin, Irvington in Portland, Oregon, Hackney in London: just mentioning the names of these neighbourhoods immediately rings a bell among locals. Indeed, sometimes even mentioning a number or compass point arouses a sense of place, like with the fourth arrondissement in Paris or the West End in London. Neighbourhoods have always been a crucial component of good cities. Yet they do not allow for easy classification, either in terms of size or any other measure. The names of neighbourhoods often refer to geography, especially if the landscape provides a clear marker, like with islands (KNSM-eiland in Amsterdam, Roosevelt Island in New York, Île de la Cité in Paris), or elevations (Beacon Hill in Boston, or Highgate in London). Yet neighbourhoods are also about atmosphere, locality, quality of place. Of course, a neighbourhood always has to have some kind of spatial delineation and has to be part of a larger urban whole. We are looking for the particular qualities that make neighbourhoods feel like good places to live in. One could see a neighbourhood *as a cohesive spatial entity within a city* but that is still quite formal and does not bring out the idea of a community, however loose. Alternatively, one could think of neighbourhoods as *loosely knitted communities of place*, as geographically localized social networks, accessible and usable for those living in the area. Avoiding the term 'community', we think that good neighbourhoods stand out for their particular 'ecologies' of interrelated places and services; places that people appreciate across social and cultural divides, and services that help people find their way, help them navigate the city. An urban neighbourhood always harbours diversity. Or as Jane Jacobs put it: '[Great cities] are not like suburbs, only denser. They differ from towns and suburbs in basic ways, and one of these is that cities are, by definition, full of strangers.'[4]

Urban geographers and urban sociologists have been fascinated by the social meaning of neighbourhoods for decades. The old and hoary question is that of so-called 'neighbourhood effects'. Does the neighbourhood make people better or worse off—often defined in economic terms—than they would have been if only their personal characteristics are taken into consideration? The fact that poor and rich people live in poor and rich neighbourhoods does not necessarily mean that the neighbourhood has *caused* this difference in personal wealth (or lack thereof). It may also indicate the result of 'sorting' or 'selection'.[5] The balance between neighbourhood and selection effects remains an unresolved issue in the literature. In this book, we will not go into this debate. We will, however, show that there are successful examples of urban interventions where a strong environmental record is combined with an improved social mix of inhabitants and users.

Putting forward neighbourhoods in the context of the climate crisis links the level of the planetary ecological challenge to that of a scale at which ordinary people and their immediate networks can be empowered to help deliver the answers. We build on a crucial insight from *The Weight of Cities*, which reveals that we can organize cities in such a way that they only require a tenth of the energy requirements of today's average. But we cannot achieve this without changing our lifestyles. We will need to create the preconditions for a 'good urban way of life' and neighbourhoods are a crucial focus in this strategy. They are, first of all, built up of a mix of functions, which can lower the overall energy requirements by a factor two or more. Moreover, when building proper *functionally mixed* neighbourhoods is combined with attention to densification, energy-efficient buildings, new energy systems (shifting from coal, oil and gas to renewable energies and introducing district-based systems instead of organizing everything on the level of an individual unit) and behavioural change because the type of urban environment allows for a lifestyle change, the net result can be a reduction by a factor of ten of emissions and resource requirements. In addition, with

[4] J. Jacobs, *The Death and Life of Great American Cities* (New York, NY: Vintage, 2016), p. 30.

[5] See, for instance: W.J. Wilson, *The Truly Disadvantaged: The Inner City, the Underclass and Public Policy* (Chicago, IL: University of Chicago Press, 1987); M. van Ham et al., eds., *Neighbourhood Effects Research: New Perspectives* (Dordrecht: Springer, 2012). For a brief overview of the literature: see Chapter 4 of E. Buitelaar, A. Weterings, and R. Ponds, *Cities, Economic Inequality and Justice: Reflections and Alternative Perspectives* (London: Routledge, 2017).

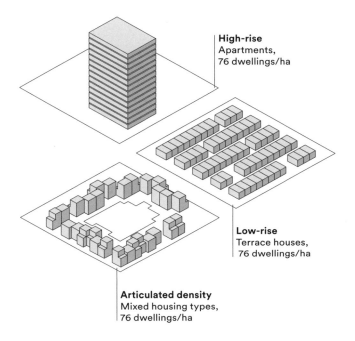

High-rise
Apartments,
76 dwellings/ha

Low-rise
Terrace houses,
76 dwellings/ha

Articulated density
Mixed housing types,
76 dwellings/ha

Fig. 1.3 ↑ Different spatial scenarios, yet similar densities per hectare: a lot depends on the type of housing that is built. Adapted from: H. Meyer, J. Westrik, and M. Hoekstra, *Stedebouwkundige regels voor het bouwen* (Nijmegen: SUN, 2008).

such a neighbourhood-based strategy planetary issues can be addressed in direct connection with the everyday concerns of many citizens who now sometimes feel that addressing the climate crisis happens at the expense of addressing issues that they are concerned about, such as affordability, moist and draught, security, and the well-being of their children.

We argue that the ambition to create climate-neutral cities should be combined with creating really pleasant urban environments, where homes, workplaces, and services are brought together in new ways. Higher densities are a concern, but *The Weight of Cities* shows that these densities do not have to be outrageous. For new districts, city planners can aim for 10,000 to 15,000 people per square kilometre, which is well below the average of that of the Parisian arrondissements. Moreover, the lowest energy and resource requirements come from an 'articulated density' → Fig. 1.3, which is a varied pattern of densities, in some areas up to 20,000 inhabitants per square kilometre, in others with a much lower density, and always alternated with green spaces. With articulated density, cities would still comprise areas of lower density but contain well-connected 'nodes' with a much higher density of residents, jobs, services and urban amenities.

All in all, sustainability and quality of life can very well go hand in hand, but only if we combine reaching climate targets with a conscious effort to (re)build our cities from the neighbourhoods up.

Forms of Urbanization

We pit urban neighbourhoods against the two forms of formalized urbanization that dominated the twentieth century in the West. First, there is *the modernist high-rise in the twentieth century*. Originating in the work of the modern architectural movement of the 1920s and 1930s, it led to a building boom in the post-war decades in which, in response to urgent housing shortages, large strips of high-rise and superblocks were built, in particular in North American and European cities. Interestingly, it was a style of building that was in vogue both in the communist countries of Eastern Europe and in the capitalist countries of the time.

It is easy to forget, but the idea of the 'high-rise in the park' was born out of idealism. Modern architecture and urban planning were to provide a *Neue Heimat* for the open society, as the German social-democrats described it.[6] It was based on the idea that modernism would lead to better, healthier living, using the latest insights in building technique (steel construction, reinforced concrete, prefab production, and using geometrical form) to build higher volumes at an industrial pace. The fascination with new technology, the emergence of the automobile, the possibility of high-rise and flat roofs, led to a fully grown 'imaginary' of a 'city of tomorrow', promoted by key figures of the modern movement in architecture, such as Le Corbusier and Gropius, and disseminated via world expos and commercial advertisements.[7] Moreover, in the post-war years, modernism was also pitted against the fascist preference for classical and traditional architecture with its ornaments and historical references. Modernist architecture was seen as the architecture of freedom, both in the East and in the West. A case in point is Regent Park → p. 148, the Toronto neighbourhood that we will discuss in detail later on in this book. It was literally framed as a 'community of the future' when it was under construction in the 1940s and 1950s. Streets were eradicated to make place for superblocks and high-rise, and a first generation of tenants, happy to have homes in the first place, moved in.

Modernist high-rise, with its standardized, industrial production process, made it possible to build apartments in great numbers at a time of severe housing shortages in the post-war era. Moreover, in many cities the introduction of modern, geometrically organized apartment blocks was combined with an attempt to create a socially mixed neighbourhood. An example is Pendrecht in Rotterdam, the Netherlands, designed by one of the few recognized female modernists, Lotte Stam-Beese, where working-class tenants lived around the corner from schoolmasters, shopkeepers, and business administrators. It was only later, after some two generations of tenants, that the social mix evaporated, and the neighbourhood started to lose its appeal. In other places, such as in the case of Stuyvesant Town, well-positioned on the edge of Manhattan's Lower East Side, the modernist high-rise

[6] A. Lepik and H. Strobl, eds., *Die Neue Heimat (1950–1982): Eine sozialdemokratische Utopie und ihre Bauten* (Munich: Architekturmuseum der TUM and DETAIL, 2019).

[7] R.W. Rydell, *World of Fairs: The Century-of-Progress Expositions* (Chicago: University of Chicago Press, 1993).

Fig. 1.4 ↑ Cabrini-Green public housing, Chicago.

Fig. 1.5 ↑ Pruitt-Igoe public housing, St. Louis.

is still providing good housing, be it increasingly at unaffordable prices for most people. But probably its enduring quality has a lot to do with its location in the midst of the urban fabric of the Lower East Side. Inhabitants of Stuyvesant Town could 'piggyback' on the many shops that its surroundings had to offer, full of breakfast places, coffee shops, grocery shops, dry cleaners, and the like.

All too often, the standardized modernist building style was adopted by real estate developers going for a quick profit, producing housing units to schedule, instead of building proper neighbourhoods. It resulted in bad quality of housing, with noisy and moist housing situations. Unfortunately, this was often combined with a lack of care for the social diversity of the tenants as well as a lack of budget for maintenance and supervision. Even well-built structures cannot prevent a downward spiral when too many people struggling with health, social, or psychological problems (or a combination of those) share corridors and elevators, let alone badly constructed ones. No collective building will remain pleasant when cleaning and maintenance is not organized and funded properly. Together, this created the archetypical images of modern housing blocks unfit for living. In the end, planners started to reject this style of building, probably most symbolically marked by the dynamiting of the Pruitt-Igoe projects → Fig. 1.5 in Saint Louis in 1972.[8] The Bijlmermeer in Amsterdam was built in the 1960s and 1970s and subsequently partially knocked down in the 1990s and 2000s to make way for low- and medium-height buildings. And Regent Park, Toronto, which started as a 'neighbourhood of the future', was completely restructured, bringing back streets and mixed use since 2006 with a new, grounded sense of a neighbourhood as a result.

The worst combination was where the high modernist style of urban design was employed in combination with satellite towns, adding distance to the inhuman layout of buildings and their surroundings, such as in the French banlieues, some British estates, or in the Swedish satellite towns around Stockholm, such as Rinkeby, Tensta or Akalla. Still, modernist high-rise remains the predominant style of the formal extensions

[8] C. Jencks, *The Language of Post-Modern Architecture* (New York, NY: Rizzoli, 1984).

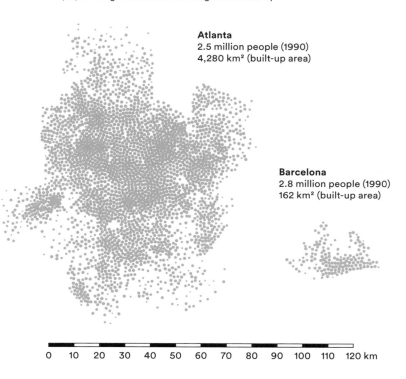

Atlanta
2.5 million people (1990)
4,280 km² (built-up area)

Barcelona
2.8 million people (1990)
162 km² (built-up area)

0   10   20   30   40   50   60   70   80   90   100   110   120 km

Fig. 1.6 ↑ The built-up areas of Atlanta and Barcelona illustrate the difference between urban sprawl and high-density urban development. Adapted from: A. Bertaud, *The Spatial Organization of Cities: Deliberate Outcome or Unforeseen Consequence?* (Berkeley, CA: University of California, Berkeley, 2004), p. 17.

to cities in countries such as China, India, Turkey, or Iran. Indeed, recently, its Chinese variation has become an export product to African countries, for instance in Kilamba New City, an 8.8 square kilometre satellite town, built some eighteen miles outside Luanda, Angola and constructed by Chinese developers as part of a money-for-oil swap.

The problem with this type of urban structure is, first of all, that it stands in the way of any sense of belonging in the neighbourhood. In these modernist high-rises, it is as if the front door of private homes opens up directly onto the anonymity of the city. It lacks the ecology of nodes, the rows of shops that allow for mingling. Second, modernist constructions do not lend themselves to easy adaptation. Residents have to do without the soft spaces that are easy to adapt and cater for new use, from easy extensions to their homes to opening small shops. Third, the modernist high-rise was part of the broader urban imaginary of the 'functional city', separating dwelling, work, mobility, and recreation, as if the costs of mobility would never be a problem. This has impacted the lives of many on a daily basis. Nothing was easy, everything required traveling. In the meantime, we should know better. Modernist high-rise is part of an urban configuration based on the enthusiasm for the automobile. The car as a technology of freedom. In fact, it created a nightmare for many. While the initial projects were based on the idea of a male breadwinner and a wife staying at home, we now should really abandon this model of urbanization. Environmental consequences of moving about may not have been on the radar at the time but now they are. The social consequences are similarly obvious. Now we face the task of coming to terms with the unintended effects of all the modernist urban development based on what was once a technology of freedom. We should stop building cities with this design and try our best to transform the areas that have been built in this tradition into properly functioning neighbourhoods.

The second form of formalized urbanization is *the suburb*; again, a twentieth-century invention. The original idea behind the suburb was benign, idealistic, even. Ebenezer Howard came up with the idea of a *garden city* in the final years of the nineteenth century, but this subsequently was the inspiration for all sorts of ideas about new settlements beyond the city's perimeter.[9] For Howard, the new urban form of a garden city was part and parcel of an ideal of a new social life and a restructuring of the economy, allowing it to work for people rather than the other way around. The original title of his book reflected this: *A Peaceful Path to Real Reform* (1898).

Another urban utopian thinker of that time, Frank Lloyd Wright, best known for his iconic buildings such as Fallingwater in Pennsylvania and the Guggenheim Museum in New York, took a different route. Like Howard, he despised the city of the time—which he referred to as a 'fibrous tumour'—but he had an even more extreme form of urban decentralization in mind: that of the *broadacre city*. At the core of this concept is not the community, as in Howard's garden city concept, but the individual family home sat on a large plot and customized to the individualized lifestyle. It would mean a scattered low-density urban morphology facilitated by a network of superhighways.[10] With the emergence of the automobile, his idea for a new urban morphology was appropriated by commercial entrepreneurs who bought land and subsequently sold small plots with the characteristic detached or semi-detached houses in the regions around the major cities on land that had been used for agriculture.

As the economy grew, the automobile became affordable and the growing middle classes flocked to the new types of urbanization. Now motorways connected new housing in single-family homes in culs-de-sac to the cities. Later this type of urbanization produced the out-of-town shopping mall for 'functional shopping' and still later the 'edge cities' of (back)offices which led to an overall de-densification of cities and a major increase in the daily mileage of the average worker. This developer-led suburban pattern of urbanization, with its high dependency on automobility, now spread out over the planet, led urban sociologist Roger Keil to speak of our 'suburban planet'.[11] It is well documented that suburbanization leads to a spatial sorting of social groups. Initially, those who could afford it left the socially and racially mixed inner cities but, more recently, poverty has spread to

[9] E. Howard, *Garden Cities of To-Morrow* (Cambridge, MA: MIT Press, 1965).

[10] R. Fishman, *Urban Utopias in the Twentieth Century: Ebenezer Howard, Frank Lloyd Wright, and Le Corbusier* (Cambridge, MA: MIT Press, 1982).

[11] R. Keil, *Suburban Planet: Making the World Urban from the Outside In* (Hoboken, NJ: Wiley, 2017).

the suburbs because housing closer to the city cores is becoming unaffordable for lower-income groups. The European Environment Agency reports over sixty negative effects associated with urban sprawl, among them a large number of environmental aspects, including effects on hygiene, landscape, and flora and fauna; economic aspects such as traffic congestion costs, public service costs; and social aspects, including health problems.[12] All in all, it is hard to see how the suburb can fit any model of a sustainable urban future.

Neither of the two types of patterned urbanization is consistent with urban futures that are both environmentally sustainable and socially just. The high-rise in the park seemingly has a high density but the actual high-rising buildings are nearly always combined with large tracts of surrounding space left vacant or to be used for parking, driving (motorways, relief roads), or as underdefined green space to compensate for the high density in the built form. The fact that suburbs are spread out in space requires stunning numbers of linear meters of sewage systems, roads, electricity and fibre cables, water and gas pipes. Suburbs are an ecological catastrophe not only because of their low density but because this goes hand in hand with an almost total car dependency for nearly all practical purposes, from shopping to bringing kids to school to commuting to work. And in addition to all those environmental concerns we already mentioned the social consequences of these urban models of the twentieth century. We feel it is time to move on and help create urban environments that bring with them a new sense of a good urban way of living.

We will need to help develop proper neighbourhoods that cater to both housing and work, that have amenity for various forms of recreation, and make part of our mobility requirements redundant. This can be done. For example, the neighbourhood of Nordhavn → p. 86, in the Danish capital of Copenhagen, comes a long way in that regard, with one job for every inhabitant, ample recreational space, and a 'green loop'—a new low-carbon mobility system.

Obviously, there is never a one-size-fits-all solution to the problems of sustainable urbanization. Still, we argue that urban neighbourhoods of medium density, a mixed use, and social diversity come a long way to reaching our climate targets. But in terms of urban strategy, we do not merely argue that urban neighbourhoods can be the cornerstone of achieving climate-neutral cities; we think they can also be an imaginary to rethink modernist high-rise and suburban environments. The agenda laid out in this book suggests that urban neighbourhoods can be good for more than just fighting the climate crisis. They can help create cities that are more liveable and will prove to be much more enduring as they allow for adjustment over time. Moreover, it may guide the conversion of the current suburban landscapes.[13]

[12] See E. Henning et al., *Urban Sprawl in Europe* (Copenhagen: European Environment Agency, 2016). For alternative overviews of urban sprawl, we refer to J. Brueckner, 'Urban Sprawl: Diagnosis and Remedies', *International Regional Science Review* 23, no. 2 (2000), pp. 160–171; T. Nechyba and R. Walsh, 'Urban Sprawl', *Journal of Economic Perspectives* 18, no. 4 (2004), pp. 177–200; G. Squires, ed., *Urban Sprawl: Causes, Consequences and Policy Responses* (Washington, DC: The Urban Institute Press, 2002).

[13] P. Calthorpe and W. Fulton, *The Regional City: Planning for the End of Sprawl* (Washington, DC: Island Press, 2001); P. Calthorpe, *Urbanism in the Age of Climate Change* (Washington, DC: Island Press, 2011).

Rethinking Urbanism

We situate this plea for a neighbourhood strategy in the intellectual tradition of urbanism. Urbanism is a body of knowledge aimed at understanding urban dynamics to help create better cities. It is an interdisciplinary conversation, a particular type of thinking, connecting urban planning to sociology, economics, architecture, and urban design.[14] Urbanism is devoted to understanding how urban life evolves in a real-life context of constant pressures, of creating opportunities, of (re)appropriation, and of displacement and re-enabling. It stands out for its commitment to put this understanding of urban dynamics to use, indeed, to help create better urban environments for people to live in. How can people make themselves feel at home in the city, and use the qualities of the urban environment in terms of inspiration, prosperity, and well-being?

We see urbanism *as efforts to understand patterns of urbanization combined with the wish to help create thriving cities.* We argue that this tradition of urbanism now needs to be given a central place in our thinking about cities in these times of climate crisis. This requires a complete overhaul of modernist urbanism. The twentieth century was arguably urbanism's finest hour. Never before have architects and city planners had such an encompassing influence on how we live. Yet the record of twentieth-century urbanism is mixed, at best. We think this has to do with the political and economic naivety, if not cynicism of those modernist urbanists. After all, it was not just the power of their ideas that made them so impactful; they fitted the system of their time, with politicians eager to reach quantitative goals and developers seeing ample opportunity to earn money building their intellectual creations. To be able to deliver on a world of neighbourhoods we need a new type of urbanism, one that is able to combine insights into how people want to live or can live with the technological possibilities that most people are not aware of. And also based on a new politics that recoups the ability to listen to people, understand their needs, and combines this with a zeal to deliver solutions that work for people living in cities.

It depends, in fact, which century's approach we prefer. If we approach the 'climate proofing' of cities in the technology-oriented, technocratic way, with a predominance *for* and *of* scientific experts, we prolong the modernist urbanism of the twentieth century. Alternatively, we can start from the ambitious climate targets but actively seek to combine this with making good urban neighbourhoods, like the ones from the nineteenth century, that are not only more liveable and pleasant but also allow for people to go through the day much easier—get to work, pick up kids from school, hang out, be inspired, and relax.

There is no shortage of concepts that suggest delivering on a positive future for cities in times of the climate crisis: eco-cities, green cities, sustainable cities. The list is long and can be extended. Yet, as the

[14] K. Lynch, *The Image of the City* (Cambridge, MA: MIT Press, 1960); L. Mumford, *The City in History: Its Origins, Its Transformations, and Its Prospects* (New York, NY: Harcourt, Brace & World, 1961); R. Sennett, *Building and Dwelling: Ethics for the City* (London: Penguin Books, 2018); S. Zukin, *The Cultures of Cities* (Oxford: Wiley-Blackwell, 1995).

above makes clear, our worry is that most of these texts are accompanied by a strong belief in new technologies, 'smart' or otherwise. In the drive to insulate our homes, bring down energy consumption and regenerate waste, we potentially produce, with the best intentions, more urban fabric unfit for habitation in an era of climate crisis.

We can only avoid this *technocratic fallacy* if we are willing to try and make cities that are both ecologically and socially excellent and listen to and work with the people that live in them. If so, we still need to seriously reflect on the epistemological underpinnings of contemporary urbanism. If we just proceed, we run the risk of trying to solve the ecological crisis with the very modernist tools that produced it in the first place. If, on the other hand, we are willing to reflect on the underpinnings of our urbanism, we can indeed conceive of a strategy to rebuild our cities successfully from the neighbourhood up.

Sometimes we now hear that we need to 'climate proof' our cities, retrofit homes with new equipment to cut energy demand. We agree that cutting CO_2 emissions is of paramount importance. But we need to connect this endeavour to taking care of a better environment for the people living in those cities. Sometimes there seems to be a faint echo of Le Corbusier's famous functionalist metaphor of the 'home as a machine for living' in today's use of terms like 'targets', 'smart buildings', or 'metabolic flows'. The challenge we face is not captured in the language of 'upgrades' and the installation of new 'smart' technological systems to improve the 'performance' of the city. We think that a deep reflection on the failures of modernist urbanism calls for a deep reorientation. One in which we equally focus on making the city more humane.[15] If we don't, we may end up with the continuation of modernist urbanism in a green disguise. We argue for a reappreciation of the city as a spontaneous order, that is, a stable set of relations that emerges from collective interactions; they are 'the result of human action but not of human (technocratic) design'.[16]

The Neighbourhood as a Spontaneous Order

'Home is where your credit is good at the corner store', writes the Indian novelist Suketu Mehta in *Maximum City*, acknowledging how important a neighbourhood is for us to feel at home in big cities such as New York or Mumbai. The neighbourhood is the domain of 'sort of knowing' each other. In well-functioning neighbourhoods we share a collective space, we keep an eye on each other in a non-intrusive way. We know our grocery store, our bakery, the corner pub.

Or take the example of the neighbourhood where one of us lives. It is just an ordinary street. Every morning the shoe repairman opens his shop at 8.30. He cycles in from Zoetermeer, a Dutch new town, some twenty kilometres away. He and his wife moved out of the city decades ago, to live in an affordable single-family home in the suburbs. 'Sometimes I miss it here, and I would like to move back. But we can no longer afford a home here; it has all become too

[15] K. Pålsson, *How to Design Human Cities* (Berlin: DOM Publishers, 2017).

[16] S. Ikeda, 'The City Cannot Be a Work of Art', *Cosmos and Taxis* 4, no. 2/3 (2017), pp. 79–86.

Fig. 1.7 ↑ The Reinkenstraat in The Hague's neighbourhood of Duinoord.

expensive', he says with a wry smile. He may no longer live here but he still is a central figure in the neighbourhood of Duinoord, in The Hague, the Netherlands. If you have an extra key made for visitors and wonder how to get it to them, you can leave it with him for the visitors to pick up. Next door is Mesut's Turkish barbershop, with its dark brown interior, complete with sturdy chesterfield seats. Greenish light spreads from their English-style banker's lamps. Here they take trimming your beard to a completely new level and tell you the latest gossip from the neighbourhood and the Mediterranean in the meantime. Two blocks down is Ad Schilperoort, the hardware store that seemingly has everything you could possibly need in your household: a stepladder, a new broom or that the single plug and drill bit you need to hang a picture on the crumbling wall at home. Although they make a living out of selling utensils, they also have a drawer behind the counter with some tools for you to borrow; 'If you need it just for this one time, it doesn't make sense to buy, does it?' At one in the afternoon, Colette opens its doors. A second-hand bookshop, where the books are stacked so high and in such seemingly unstable piles that you sometimes hesitate to go in. But you are always curious about new arrivals. Every couple of weeks the owner creates a new shop window to match the theme of the day.

The Reinkenstraat → Fig. 1.7 is an example of a street that gives a neighbourhood its 'node', in terms of Kevin Lynch.[17] Real estate agents know all too well

[17] Lynch, *Image of the City*, 1960.

how important such streets are. An apartment may be spacious, and nice oak floors and panelled doors may help sell it, but people also look at the surroundings. That is the scale of the neighbourhood, the next scale up from the home, the stepping stone between home and city, between intimacy and anonymity, between the home as the domain of tracksuit bottoms and flip flops and that of the urban performance in suits, uniform, or leather jackets.

We all know urban life can be rough at times, but a good neighbourhood creates personal resilience. Cities are made up of neighbourhoods like a checkerboard is made up of fields. We think it is time for a reappraisal of the districts, the arrondissements, the *Bezirke*, the quarters that make cities. A good neighbourhood makes people feel at ease. If the kitchen is the heart of the home, the neighbourhoods are the nerves of the city. This is where you can relax. But not all neighbourhoods have the quality of Duinoord, The Hague. Indeed, most people are likely to live in neighbourhoods that lack those special qualities. However, we feel we can use these descriptions, as they may function as an 'imaginary' of what sort of qualities we would ideally share, what sort of services and infrastructure to aim for.

Richard Sennett argues that good urban environments are where *ville* (built form) and *cité* (social fabric) go together.[18] We agree. That too is part of the rich tradition of urbanism we can draw on in redefining urbanism in light of today's climate crisis. Looking around, it seems that we have lost the art of urbanism, that we build housing rather than that we create new neighbourhoods; that we predominantly think in quantities rather than in insisting on a quality of place. We build and sell homes that require people to spend way too much time away from their loved ones; we separate people instead of helping them to connect. Alternatively, we rethink how we build cities that allow for a variety of urban lifestyles to prosper and to produce an urban environment that is sustainable in the long run. That is the challenge we want to focus on in the remainder of this chapter.

The Plea for an Ecological Urbanism

We call for a new agenda of an *ecological urbanism*. 'Ecology' has been used frequently in the urbanist literature, from the Chicago School to a range of more recent adaptations. But we want to take a next step, which we will clarify below. Ecological urbanism signals, first of all, the need to make nature an inseparable part of thinking about cities. At the moment, urbanization is basically 'building on top' of the natural environment. This echoes the modernist ideal of *tabula rasa* planning, in which the natural context was often erased to make way for the stylized geometry of modernist urban forms. But in a more practical sense, this tradition is still with us. Concrete is often used to provide an impenetrable 'floor' in the city, the most dramatic example being airports where many square kilometres of nature are covered in concrete. Elsewhere urbanization takes place in floodplains, hindering the flow of rivers. This approach

[18] Sennett, *Building and Dwelling*, 2018.

Fig. 1.8 ↑ Boeri's vertical forest: how ecological urbanism is often imagined.

proves to be very vulnerable in times of torrential rain, leading to flooding and disruption. The most immediate response has been the Chinese call for 'sponge cities', emphasizing the need to absorb water in the urban environment. A more profound break with modernist urbanism is the idea of nature-based solutions, in which the power and intelligence of the natural environment is taken as a starting point for finding solutions.[19] An ecological urbanism suggests that we need to take nature into account when thinking about the future of our cities.

The second dimension of an ecological urbanism refers back to its sociological usage. Way back, in the 1920s and 1930s, urbanists such as Louis Wirth, Robert E. Park, and Ernest W. Burgess introduced the ecological metaphor, emphasizing the fact that city life had the characteristics of a complex ecosystem, in which people attracted each other, or pushed others out. That approach to urban dynamics is something worth reconsidering when thinking about the neighbourhoods for the future. Well-functioning neighbourhoods have their own social ecology as well. Indeed, one of the reasons why many of the modernist high-rise environments proved to be inhabitable in the long run, has to do with that lack of such an urban dynamics, in which functions that live of each other, that complement each other, can also find a spatial expression, creating the nodes that are typical of good neighbourhoods.

The term 'ecological urbanism' has been used before, most notably in a large volume edited by Mohsen Mostafavi and Gareth Doherty.[20] We want to take a next step, providing the conceptual tools to help understand the challenges in creating neighbourhoods for the future. This requires a repositioning of the principles of urbanism. Only then can we avoid merely paying lip service to the vast ecological challenges we face, like for example in architect Stefano Boeri's 'vertical forests' → Fig. 1.8. This new type of building is a commercial success but in essence just adds a visible layer of green to an urban fabric that is basically unaltered. This amounts to 'greenwashing' the modernist tradition, varnishing buildings and locations to improve the marketability of real estate.

Here, we use the term ecological urbanism emphasizing the new agenda, combining seeing nature and the care for natural resources as an inseparable part of urbanization (nature-based solutions) on the one hand, and conceptualizing neighbourhoods

[19] N. Frantzeskaki et al., 'Nature-based Solutions for Urban Climate Change Adaptation: Linking Science, Policy, and Practice Communities for Evidence-based Decision-making', *BioScience* 69, no. 6 (2019), pp. 455–466.

[20] M. Mostafavi and G. Doherty, eds., *Ecological Urbanism* (Cambridge, MA: Harvard Graduate School of Design/Baden, CH: Lars Müller Publishers, 2016).

(and beyond that cities), in a naturalistic way, as 'ecosystems' and 'habitats' on the other.[21] An ecological urbanism thus gives new meaning to the goals we want to achieve. Ecology is used to emphasize the need to look at components of the urban in an integrated perspective, looking for ways in which they can create true ecosystems of elements that reinforce each other in producing good city life, appreciating the subtle ways in which neighbourhoods actually become nice places to live in. We argue for an approach in which the 'ecological' is bolted *into*, not onto urbanism.

An ecological urbanism starts from a recognition of how cities and nature are fundamentally intertwined. And this requires us to rethink some of the very fundamentals of making cities. First, we need to reconsider building materials. We are all but locked into a style of conceiving and building cities that leads to extremely high CO_2 emissions. Reinforced concrete was (and still is) a favourite material for buildings and infrastructure alike, all because of its strength and, literally, malleability. Concrete was used to make pavements and surfaces for industry and airports. But the production of concrete, steel and cement is also a major source of CO_2 emissions. This basically requires us to rethink the materials we use to build and improve our cities. This is by no means easy.

Moreover, we need to reconsider our commitment to a certain type of knowledge. Behind the materiality of today's cities are ideas. Indeed, the preference for concrete and steel stems from an intellectual conviction. Modernist urbanism had a preference for geometry and tabula rasa, erasing existing landscapes to create the optimal spatial conditions for designed freedom. It was deeply felt at the time, and one should keep in mind that it also made sense: modern architecture and urban design were conceived as an answer to the unhealthy conditions of urban slum life at the time. And, arguably, this process of slum development was regarded as a *natural* process, an 'urban cancer', in the words of Lewis Mumford, against which the modernists tried to find a remedy. Hence, in that sense, for good reason. However, it suggested a superiority of analytical thinking over a type of knowledge that sees urban life as something that is growing, changing and constantly shifting. It suggested that a forceful break with the past was the logical next step, also in light of the need to speed up in times of serious housing shortages. The idea of the modernist visionary, with privileged access to knowledge, also suggested a limited openness to discussion, to debate and to amendments, indeed, to politics. The modernist fallacy was epistemological in the sense that it suggested a general law, a calculated optimum. The suggestion that we could and should aim for a type of urban solutions that were universal both in their claims to truth and in their applicability. It is this modernist conceptualization that gave us all these more or less identical high-rise developments, from the New York super-blocks to the high-rise in Qom, Iran; from the *banlieue*

[21] A.W. Spirn, 'Ecological Urbanism: A Framework for the Design of Resilient Cities', in *The Ecological Design and Planning Reader*, ed. F.O. Ndubisi (Washington, DC: Island Press, 2014), pp. 557–571; M. Gandy, 'From Urban Ecology to Ecological Urbanism: An Ambiguous Trajectory', *Area* 47, no. 2 (2015), pp. 150–154.

of Paris to the satellite towns of Stockholm. But there was no eye for detail (the fact that Corbusier's 'modular man' was based on the size of a European man did not hinder him from sticking to this standard when building in Chandigarh, India). Neither was there an ear for the struggle of people to try and make a living in a context that cost them energy instead of relieving them. Moreover, there was no anticipation that people may find modernist solutions less than optimal. Consequently, altering the modernist fabric proved to be very difficult, sometimes impossible. An ecological urbanism would fundamentally break with this idea of a theoretically and conceptually derived optimum and would instead aim to create knowledge that would allow stakeholders—including citizens—to find the best solutions, building on the insights of experts.

So, for us, an ecological urbanism is more than just a combination of the insights into what we need to do to cope with the climate crisis with the rich understanding of what makes for thriving cities. We think it calls for a new approach to planning, one that is much more appreciative of context, of how people make a living in cities, and definitely much more appreciative of how cities are fundamentally about movement and change, both of materials and natural flows as of people and their values. This idea of the city as a living organism, that should be understood against the background of its capacity to harness flows and to create a built environment that helps to express its collective values, is an important correction to all those that think that there is an optimum, an ideal city.

Ecological urbanism, then, is the theoretical approach to urbanization that combines the accumulated understanding of the physical side of the built environment with the understanding of social interaction in cities. It brings together the wisdom of its residents with the insights of experts and it, ultimately, seeks to be the new normative underpinning of a vibrant debate on what makes for thriving cities. It hopes to define a new leitmotiv for policymakers and city makers to further their quest to make better cities. As Richard Sennett has reminded us so often, good urban spaces are the product of an evolutionary understanding of the quality of place. If ecological urbanism is to be about the mastery of making better places that reduce our ecological footprint, then we should not start from the presumption that we 'know' what to do, but that we are finding out what can and should be done. It is an attitude, a 'way of seeing' that is appreciative of shifts and turns. It is more about wisdom than it is about fixed parameters and general laws, more about understanding complexities than a search for significant correlations. 'A good-quality environment is one which can be repaired', argues Sennett, and that should also apply to the new 'climate-proof' neighbourhoods and retrofits that are currently underway.[22]

[22] R. Sennett, 'Rupture, Accretion and Repair', in *Shaping Cities in an Urban Age*, ed. R. Burdett and P. Rode (London: Phaidon Press, 2018), pp. 128–135.

New Neighbourhood Ecologies

We think neighbourhoods should be the cornerstones in this new ecological urbanism. Neighbourhoods have always emerged in cities, some with good reputations, some less so. One of the fascinations has always been what makes a neighbourhood a separate entity. What do people in a neighbourhood have in common? When do people really feel at home? Historically, human geographers have dealt with the issue what determines the character of a place, such as a type of economic activity as in New York's Meatpacking District or harbour districts all over the world. Even more attention has been given to the social background of residents to describe the character of places, such as with many of the traditional immigrant neighbourhoods, which played a central role in the Chicago School of Sociology (for instance, Burgess' model of concentric zones). Think of Polish Downtown in Chicago or Chinatown or Little Italy in New York. But we always found that the cohesion in these neighbourhoods went deeper than sharing a job, a religion, or land of origin. These neighbourhoods were communities, where people knew each other well, helped each other out, argued, surely, or gossiped about one another. Yet, all in all, they enacted that social behaviour that created the neighbourhood as the sphere of 'sort of knowing' each other. On a less idealistic note, these tight-knit communities sometimes contradicted the very idea of '*Stadtluft macht frei*'[23] because social control was high, and the village was quite literally back in the city.

Back in the 1920s and 1930s, the Chicago School showed how cities function like ecosystems, with neighbourhoods where people arrive, and places where people want to move towards as soon as their economic position allows them to. In *Arrival City*, Doug Saunders showed that this holds true today as well.[24] Nearly all cities have particular neighbourhoods where migrants first arrive. And, depending on the particular qualities of these arrival cities, they find their way into the city or not. Saunders revealed that these particular qualities are about the physical possibility for intermingling, for accessible social networks, openness of the labour markets, with places that allow you to get to know your new environment and its inhabitants.[25]

To take up this challenge we coin the term *neighbourhood ecology*, which refers to those component parts (services, 'nodes' for exchange as well as more material infrastructures) that make a neighbourhood into a 'good' neighbourhood. Invoking the term 'ecology' means to emphasize that we should look at those component parts as an integrated whole. In the past, we have aimed for mixed-use or socially mixed neighbourhoods. But the point now is that we need to think of solutions that create quality because they belong together. Businesses that can feed off each other's ideas and are located close to each other create added value. Strijp-S → p. 98 is a neighbourhood in Eindhoven, the Netherlands, on the former terrain of high-tech firm Philips. Here, designers find it much easier to get access to new markets because they have manufacturing sites for fine metals around the corner. That collaboration of a design

[23] See for instance: I.M. Young, *Justice and the Politics of Difference* (Princeton, NJ: Princeton University Press, 2011).

[24] D. Saunders, *Arrival City: How the Largest Migration in History is Reshaping Our World* (New York, NY: Vintage Books, 2012).

[25] See also P. Cachola Schmal, A. Scheuermann, and O. Elser, *Making Heimat: Germany, Arrival Country* (Berlin: Hatje Cantz, 2017).

academy, places for start-ups and actual production capacity makes for an 'ecosystem' that allows them to have a greater impact. Similarly, a neighbourhood can prosper if we organize food production and consumption in such a way that it reduces the ecological footprint of our food *and* enhances the sociability of a neighbourhood. In that sense, there is a difference between smart delivery of meals to many houses to providing the spaces for small restaurants in which we can eat those meals together.

Four Dimensions of a Good Neighbourhood Ecology
In light of the challenges described above, we distinguish four dimensions to judge neighbourhood ecologies. First, its *sustainability performance*. A neighbourhood for the future should have a very low CO_2 footprint, should have a resource strategy, both in terms of construction materials and in terms of the use of resources that a neighbourhood requires for its operation. It should take on issues such as biodiversity or waste reduction and recycling strategies.

Second, a neighbourhood ecology refers to those socio-physical features of a neighbourhood that create the *conditions for sociability*. Living close to each other is no guarantee for sociability. Indeed, loneliness rates as one of the biggest social problems in cities, with dear consequences for health as well. The examples of Vauban or Duinoord, as shown above, reveal component parts of what we could call an infrastructure of conviviality.

Third, *affordability and inclusiveness*. In the past, we have seen how neighbourhoods developed into monocultures. Processes like gentrification drive the poor out of successful neighbourhoods. On the other hand, there are neighbourhoods where problems accumulate and where the new arrivals enter the city. These 'problematic' or 'weak' neighbourhoods are etched in the mental map of citizens as no-go areas. A remarkable example thereof is the case of Regent Park in Toronto. Although the neighbourhood has recovered over recent years, most Torontonians still avoid the place as they strongly associate it with crime, violence, and despair. But what this neighbourhood also shows is how a particular infrastructure can change this. In the case of Regent Park, it is the aquatic centre, which is a swimming pool so fantastic that it has been discovered by many Torontonians from outside the neighbourhood. So here a renewal strategy has created inclusiveness by placing infrastructure in the neighbourhood that makes Regent Park into a destination, rather than a place to avoid.

Fourth, we think neighbourhood ecologies should be judged in terms of their *adaptability*. A key difference between the modernist high-rise of the twentieth century and the urban neighbourhoods such as nineteenth-century Duinoord or twenty-first-century Vauban is that the modernist structures do not allow for easy adjustment while Duinoord or Vauban do. If we really want to aim for a new social quality of urban neighbourhoods, we should take into account how they can adapt to cater to new demands, new insights, new ideals.

Neighbourhood Arrangements

Describing or defining an ideal neighbourhood is one thing, realizing it is quite another. To understand how we can realize grounded neighbourhoods according to the principles of ecological urbanism, we investigate the policy arrangements that underpin successful retrofits or newly built environments. We coin the term *neighbourhood arrangement*, which is 'a temporary stabilization of the relation between *discourse*, *actors*, *resources* and *rules* in a neighbourhood to spark transformative change'.[26] Neighbourhood transformation requires a *congruent* neighbourhood arrangement in which all these four elements come together and fit.[27] Here we will discuss them one by one. The four elements are analytical tools to look into real-life examples of ecological neighbourhoods. But they also have a normative aspect: a desired content for the four concepts that, we believe, is essential or will at least increase the chances of thriving neighbourhoods.

Discourse—A discourse can be defined as an 'ensemble of notions, ideas, concepts, and categories through which meaning is given'.[28] One example is ecological urbanism itself. It is a discourse to guide neighbourhood development. If successful, its ideas start to spread and then the discourse becomes a new ideal for neighbourhood development, populated with stories of experiences on all sorts of locations. This would include inspiring the transformation of suburbs and areas dominated by modernist high-rise into neighbourhoods with a strong neighbourhood ecology. If the discourse sticks, it becomes a new shared way of talking about the qualities and challenges of urban areas. The influence of the discourse that people use when talking about reality is a huge source of power. Think of the current popularity of the 'smart city', a discourse that conceives of cities in terms of new technological apparatus, and which, often on an unconscious level, influences the way in which actors think, both about urban problems and about the solutions.

Discourses can bring together actors who do not necessarily have the same interests, such as the inhabitants of a neighbourhood, actors with financial stakes, builders, or a housing corporation. In such a 'discourse coalition', actors act in congruence because they share the same language and storylines. These storylines can be a foundational myth of a problematic past and the ways in which that past was overcome but can also be about a visit to a neighbourhood elsewhere, that functions as an exemplar for how one wants to approach the future. Each neighbourhood will have its own storylines. In Overvecht, Utrecht, very different anecdotes are being shared than in Regent Park, Toronto. Yet analytically, as researchers we can reveal the language that is recurring, or the opportunities that neighbourhoods share. All in all, we believe in the

(26) The concept of the neighbourhood arrangement was derived from the more general policy arrangement concept, as advanced in B. Arts, J. van Tatenhove, and P. Leroy, 'Policy Arrangements', in *Political Modernisation and the Environment: The Renewal of Environmental Policy Arrangements*, ed. J. van Tatenhove, B. Arts, and P. Leroy, pp. 53–69 (Dordrecht: Kluwer, 2002).

(27) The importance of congruence has been indicated by: F. Boonstra, 'Dutch Rural Policies at a Turning Point', in *Institutional Dynamics in Environmental Governance*, ed. B. Arts and P. Leroy, pp. 183–201 (Dordrecht: Springer, 2006).

(28) M.A. Hajer, *Authoritative Governance: Understanding Governance in the Age of Mediatization* (Oxford: Oxford University Press, 2009), p. 60.

power of a discourse that is coproduced with the neighbourhood and performed and reiterated by actors in and of the neighbourhood.

Actors—Discourses are always initiated and changed, produced and reproduced by actors; they cannot and must not be imposed from outside. Committed neighbourhood actors with a sense of ownership and long-term interest are pivotal to furthering an ecological urbanism. Take the long-time residents involved in the cooperatives in Vauban, who fought for alternative principles of urban design and of managing commercial functions in the neighbourhood. They have 'skin in the game', as Nicholas Nassim Taleb calls it.[29] Analyzing what makes systems resilient, Taleb reveals that decisionmakers in such situations typically bear personal risk. It is this long-term involvement— more than strict rules and regulations—that leads to attending to the long term. We agree. And what if we apply this way of thinking to the neighbourhood and aspire to have actors with 'skin in the neighbourhood'. We have come to the conclusion that the actors that have the most skin in the neighbourhood can vary. In our cases, we see statutory planners, but also real estate developers, citizen activists, managers from housing associations. But of course, it is always also about residents. They inherently have skin in the game. After all, they literally 'live' the streets of their neighbourhoods on a daily basis, they are annoyed when the neighbours' teenage or adolescent child parties until late and they typically have come to identify themselves with their 'hood'.

Citizens may have skin in the neighbourhood but they do not automatically embrace sustainable transformation. Typically, residents favour stability over change. We found an example when studying the case of Overvecht-Noord →p.178. The municipality of Utrecht has ambitious climate targets and wants to transition away from using low-caloric natural gas for heating and cooking. Just like the national government, it takes a neighbourhood-by-neighbourhood approach, with Overvecht-Noord included in the first batch of almost thirty neighbourhoods. The government introduced a strategy to kickstart this transition, invoking the metaphor of the neighbourhood as a 'test bed'.[30] An impressive amount of resources and expertise was aligned to make this happen. However, some residents of the neighbourhood, owner-occupiers who are in some cases struggling to make ends meet, reacted hesitantly and sometimes even resisted fiercely. Why should they be the proverbial guinea pigs for a change that does not directly benefit them? They have skin in their current neighbourhood, but not in the proposed decarbonization. It is only when attention is paid to good inclusive processes that one can trace what concerns inhabitants, what motivates them to opt for change. In that case, actors start to see what is in it for them and actually get 'skin in the change'.

Resources—Ecological urbanism is not a free lunch. In order for future neighbourhoods to be truly sustainable over time, we must think of ways in which a high-quality social and physical system is financially

[29] N.N. Taleb, *Skin in the Game: Hidden Asymmetries in Daily Life* (New York, NY: Random House, 2018).

[30] The initiative was officially called 'proeftuinen aardgasvrije wijken' (testing grounds for natural-gas-free neighbourhoods).

self-sustaining, or at least as much as possible. Urban planners, and other actors with 'skin' in the game, have to engage with the issue of value creation. With land development, value is added in each stage and through different activities. But truly sustainable neighbourhoods require that this value is not extracted but pays off for the inhabitants, the schools and services, and the local businesses of the neighbourhood.

There are all sorts of resources flowing through a neighbourhood. But one of particular importance is the land itself on which the neighbourhood is erected. Michael Porter introduced the concept of the *value chain*, which can also be used to capture the dynamics in land value.[31] Consequently, in this book we speak of *neighbourhood value chains*, as depicted in the image. The challenge for future neighbourhood development is to, first, *increase* the value chain and to, second, *capture* that value locally to prevent it leaking away to actors that do not invest and keep that money in the neighbourhood. 'Value capturing' is the concept often used to indicate attempts to grasp such profits and keep them there and with those that have created them in the first place.[32]

We suggest employing this concept to other resources as well. Thriving neighbourhoods are built on value capturing for neighbourhood ecologies, not on value extraction.

Rules—For discourses to take effect and materialize, enabling rules are a necessary condition. The presence of a strong and shared discourse, actors with 'skin' and with (financial) resources at their disposal are not enough. They may be hampered by overly complex and restrictive legal rules.

We firmly believe that rules that enable ecological urbanism must be *simple*. That does not mean they need to be non-restrictive. On the contrary, restrictive rules can be very helpful in making transitions happen. Take the example of the global ban on the use of chlorofluorocarbons (CFCs) to prevent a further increase of the hole in the ozone layer. What 'simple' in this context implies—among other things[33]—is rules that are not custom-made for every specific location or situation to meet social complexity. Because if you do that rules quickly become obsolete.[34] Simple rules are rules with a broader scope of application. In the context of urban and neighbourhood development, it means moving more towards *urban codes* and away from detailed land-use or zoning plans.[35] In an urban code, rules relate to categories of activities, events, land uses, and so on, rather than to specific cases thereof. In addition, such rules possess a higher degree of 'openness', which means that a given rule is permeable to trying out different solutions. An example of an open but stringent rule is the Dutch rule that prescribes that by 2025 all office space should have minimal energy performance

[31] M.E. Porter, *The Competitive Advantage: Creating and Sustaining Superior Performance* (New York City, NY: Free Press, 1985).

[32] See for instance: D. Muñoz Gielen and E. van der Krabben, *Public Infrastructure, Private Finance: Developer Obligations and Responsibilities* (Abingdon: Routledge, 2019).

[33] S. Moroni et al., 'Simple Rules for Complex Urban Problems: Toward Legal Certainty for Spatial Flexibility', *Journal of Planning Education and Research* 40, no. 3 (2020), pp. 320–331.

[34] R.A. Epstein, 'The Promise and Pitfalls of Simple Rules', *Constitutional Political Economy* no. 9 (1998), pp. 151–161.

[35] N. Alfasi and J. Portugali, 'Planning Rules for a Self-Planned City', *Planning Theory* 6, no. 2 (2007), pp. 164–182; S. Moroni, 'Planning, Liberty and the Rule of Law', *Planning Theory* 6, no. 2 (2007), pp. 146–163.

DISCOURSE	Ensemble of ideas, concepts, and categories through which meaning is given; shared language and storylines
ACTORS	Sense of ownership, long-term interest; knowing the neighbourhood
RESOURCES	Financial sustainability; neighbourhood value chain
RULES	Urban code; simplicity and stability

Fig. 1.9 ↑ Neighbourhood arrangement.

(i.e., a minimal energy label) if its owners want to continue to use or let it as an office. Energy measures to be taken are neither specified nor prescribed. Insulation improvement, alternative energy sources, even transformation into a different use, such as housing, are all on the table. The investor can then decide which investments are most efficient and whether the office is worth the investments, given market demand.

We summarize the four elements of the concept of neighbourhood arrangement in → Fig. 1.9. Using the example of a small business in electric vehicles in Utrecht we will also illustrate how we suggest using the concept of neighbourhood arrangement.

We Drive Solar → Fig. 1.10 is a business initiative that started in the neighbourhood of Lombok in the city of Utrecht, the Netherlands. It was initiated by Lombok resident and internet entrepreneur Robin Berg. He started with promoting internet access in the neighbourhood but gradually became interested in how he could provide a collective infrastructure to improve the quality of life in the neighbourhood. Berg initiated a neighbourhood value chain introducing a network of solar panels on schools and public buildings and, still later, hooked them up with a fleet of 200 electric vehicles. This network linked car batteries to solar panels in order to store electricity in times of peak production (particularly during summer days). It improved the matching of energy demand and supply. The system was built on a simple rule based on the postal code, which allowed We Drive Solar to share the electricity generated with the participants as long as they lived close to the location where the solar panels were positioned.

In March 2019, King Willem-Alexander of the Netherlands opened the world's first bidirectional charging station of We Drive Solar in Lombok. A total of 145 of such stations are to open up over the next few years around the entire city of Utrecht. A bidirectional charging station not only allows for charging but also for discharging car batteries for domestic energy use. And more importantly, it shows how a neighbourhood can get much broader improvements off the ground.

We Drive Solar is imaginative in many respects. Here is an entrepreneur with public goals who, because of his imagination,

Fig. 1.10 ↑ In front of a high school in Lombok, a neighbourhood in Utrecht, stands a car from the We Drive Solar fleet. The solar panels on the roof of the building can be linked to car batteries.

came up with an initiative that cuts across well-embedded disciplinary divides: the initiative combines mobility with electricity generation; collective storage with individual energy use. Berg had a discourse of an alternative future, in which renewable energy was the new normal. Building upon the 'can do' entrepreneurial appeal, he assembled a range of actors, building a coalition of actors with their base in various organizations. They were a true discourse coalition, all together in their wish to achieve something extraordinary. However, in pursuing their aims, Berg and his 'partners in crime' had to overcome the constraints put before them by a detailed and complex legal system: 'Because everything has been organized and regulated so precisely, change is virtually impossible. If you want to do something that is challenging or exceptional, you find the law in your way', Berg argues.[36] For instance, network operators are not allowed to store electricity, as that would qualify them as electricity providers, something they are not allowed to be. In addition, they are not allowed to make agreements with consumers about storing electricity in return for some compensation. Berg and his colleagues could eventually make use of a specific European experimental status for innovations to circumvent restrictions.

This is something that also affects the future of ecological urbanism in the broader sense. Based on imagination and discourse, a coalition of actors came together that now inspires neighbourhoods all over the Netherlands. However, this could never have been successful if this experiment had not been given permission to work around the rules; other initiatives after this would benefit from simple rules that would make room for alternative solutions within them rather than around them.[37] In the case of We Drive Solar, a new value chain could emerge, allowing for a collective system of value capturing enhancing the quality of life of the people living and working in the neighbourhood.

Using the twin concepts of 'neighbourhood ecology' and 'neighbourhood arrangement', in the remainder of this book we will try and shed light upon ways to further a new ecological urbanism to create thriving cities from the neighbourhood up.

[36] S. Bouter, 'Energietransitie? De wet werkt tegen', *NRC Handelsblad*, 21 March 2019, p. 2; translation by the authors.

[37] This complies with the argument made by V. Castán Broto and H. Bulkeley, 'A Survey of Urban Climate Change Experiments in 100 Cities', *Global Environmental Change* 23, no. 1 (2013), pp. 92–102 and by J. Evans, A. Karvonen, and R. Raven, eds., *The Experimental City* (London: Routledge, 2016).

2 Scanning Neighbourhoods for the Future

Augustenborg
Malmö, Sweden

PREVIOUS USE
Housing

CONSTRUCTION TIME
1998–2002

POPULATION
3,900

HOMES
1,850

AREA
33 hectares

→ Heavy rainfalls used to flood Augustenborg's streets, homes, and offices, but a drainage system of open conduits (━), pipes (—), manholes (●), and several water retention areas has addressed that recurring problem and contributed to making the neighbourhood climate proof.

100 m

Fig. 2.1 ↑ Children playing with a drainage channel.

Fig. 2.2 (Next spread) Mid-rises and a retention pond for rainwater.

A Model Neighbourhood Once Again —

Augustenborg, originally built shortly after the Second World War, became an exemplary eco-neighbourhood between 1998 and 2002. It had been one of Malmö's first public housing developments after the war and had quickly become an exemplar for other neighbourhoods to follow. At the time, Augustenborg was proud to be almost self-sufficient in energy, but we would now frown upon its fossil-fuelled power plant that burned five tons of coal an hour. The area fell into decline in the 1960s and 1970s. By the 1980s, those who could afford it had moved out of the damp and poorly insulated apartments, leaving many dwellings vacant. The drainage system had aged, and so the neighbourhood flooded frequently. Crises would emerge when, during heavy rainfalls, untreated sewage water ran through the streets and into people's homes and offices. As a response, the City of Malmö implemented Ekostaden Augustenborg, between 1998 and 2002. The aim was to make Augustenborg climate proof—both adaptation-wise and mitigation-wise—and fight the social decline of the neighbourhood. Far from the expo glamour of Bo01 (→ p. 122), in Augustenborg a seemingly more modest, yet highly participatory setup unfolded in which many local residents joined the discussion on the neighbourhood's future. The intense planning process ended up in an open stormwater management system that naturally drained 90 percent of the rainwater through retention ponds, and ten hectares of green roofs. MKB, the municipal housing company, renovated its 1,600 apartments, improving the climate indoors and increasing energy efficiency by 35 percent. And Augustenborg again became an innovator when it comes to energy production, now by installing solar panels and wind turbines and by using biogas and district heating.[1]

(1) Building and Social Housing Foundation, *Eco-City Augustenborg, Sweden: Winner, World Habitat Award* (Leicestershire: Building and Social Housing Foundation, 2016). Available at: http://bit.do/fJKga (accessed 20 December 2019); City of Malmö, *Ekostaden Augustenborg*, 2016. Available at: http://bit.do/fJKge (accessed 13 May 2019); City of Malmö, *Statistikunderlag för Malmö*, 2019. Available at: http://bit.do/fJKgk (accessed 20 December 2019); City of Malmö and MKB, *Ekostaden Augustenborg: On the Way Towards a Sustainable Neighbourhood* (Malmö: City of Malmö, 2016). Available at: http://bit.do/fJKgu (accessed 20 December 2019); WWF, *Green Roofs and Innovative Water System in Augustenborg*, 2012. Available at: http://bit.do/fJKgx (accessed 14 May 2019).

'By the time the developers in Bo01 were starting to think "well, what is this?", we had the first demonstration of green roofs.'

Trevor Graham
(former manager of Ekostaden Augustenborg)

BedZED
London, United Kingdom

PREVIOUS USE
Wastewater treatment plant

CONSTRUCTION TIME
2000–2002

POPULATION
250

HOMES
100

AREA
2 hectares

→ Two-third of the construction materials used for building BedZED came from within a fifty-six-kilometre radius (●) or had been recycled.

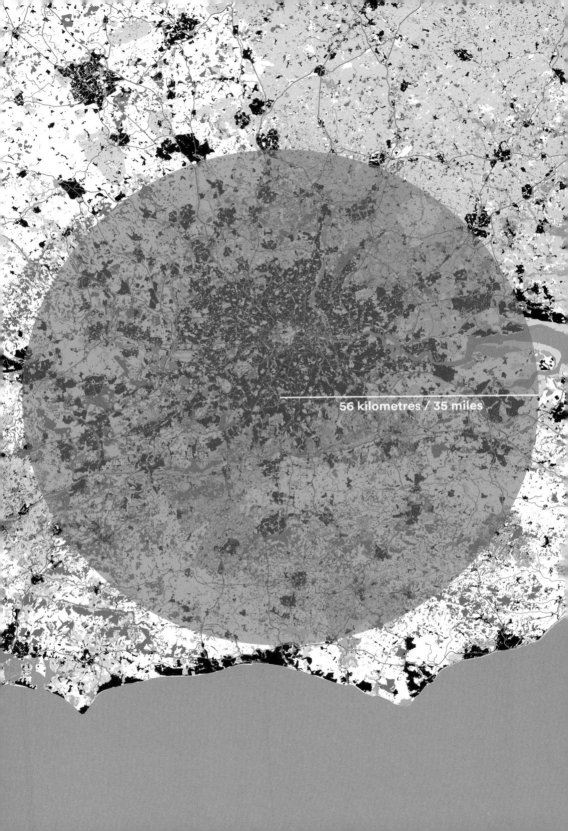

56 kilometres / 35 miles

Fig. 2.3 ↑ Single-family housing in BedZED.

Fig. 2.4 → Marching for Sutton's 'Take the one planet' challenge.

Fig. 2.5 (Next spread) Overhanging bridges connect different buildings.

The Power of the Local — It is a small neighbour-hood, yet with big sustainability ambitions: the Beddington Zero Energy Development (BedZED). Most notable is probably the origin of its <u>construction materials</u>: two-thirds of the material either came from within a fifty-six-kilometre radius or had been recycled. BedZED was built on land that was once used as a local sewage works. It now hosts a tight-knit community, consisting mostly of the original residents from the early 2000s. In 2009, it was said that BedZEDians <u>know twenty neighbours by name</u> on average; a remarkable number, compared to the average eight neighbours that residents else-where in the London Borough of Sutton tend to know. Households typically show low heating-re-lated energy consumption patterns because of the <u>passive-building techniques</u> that were used during construction. Rather than using ventilation and heating systems, it is sunlight and wind that heat up and cool homes, respectively. This is not always convenient, though: in hot summers the dwellings produce their own greenhouse effect. The pedes-trianized streets and the availability of bus and train connections facilitate a mobility pattern that emits only half the travel-related CO_2 compared to the UK average. About 17 percent of residents travel to work by car versus 49 percent on average in Sutton as a whole. <u>Water-efficient appliances</u> and <u>monitoring systems</u> have helped to build 'awareness' among residents and reduce the use of drinking water. <u>Community gardens</u> and the import of organic food from local farms stimulate local food production and consumption. And so BedZED has arguably reduced its <u>ecological footprint</u>, also because 60 percent of the waste is either recycled or composted.[2]

[2] N. Schoon, *The BedZED Story: The UK's First Large-scale, Mixed-use Eco-village* (London: BioRegional, 2016).

EcoBlock
Oakland,
California, United States

PREVIOUS USE
Housing

CONSTRUCTION TIME
2016–ongoing

POPULATION
100

HOMES
64

AREA
2 hectares

→ Retrofitting for sustainability at the block level is more efficient than doing it at the individual level. EcoBlock explores the potential of a replicable model (■), looking for a formula that both technically and financially enables a large-scale roll-out of sustainable renovations such as rain gardens (●) and rooftop energy generation (▥).

50 m

Fig. 2.6 ↑ A chestnut-covered street in EcoBlock.

Sustainable Retrofits, Ready to Roll Out — Energy and water bills often take up a significant share of household incomes. And then there's not much money left for people to invest in such measures as insulation, energy-efficient devices, and water-efficient appliances. The Oakland EcoBlock project demonstrates how to <u>combine mitigating climate change with social support</u>. In an Oakland suburb, on the eastern bank of the San Francisco Bay, plans are to have a series of homes retrofitted by a team of urban designers, architects, engineers, and social scientists and policy experts from UC Berkeley and NASA, with <u>strong participation</u> of the local community. In-home energy retrofits will spur a 58 to 63 percent <u>reduction in energy consumption</u>, and water consumption is expected to drop dramatically too, by 60 percent at least. The overall objective is to prove that <u>retrofitting at the block level</u> is cheaper and more efficient than doing it at the individual level. As such, EcoBlock provides an exemplar for sustainable renovation to be replicated across the US and beyond, a rollout that is feasible because it is 'just' established technology that is used: 'deep' energy-efficiency retrofits, solar panels, air-based heat-pumps and electric vehicles—cars, scooters, and so on. Reduced water consumption is possible, again, with a little help from efficiency measures and by <u>closing water cycles</u>— storing rainwater underground, using it in washing machines and toilets, then purifying it on-site and using it again, now as irrigation for plants and trees. Savings on utility bills will pay for the required investments. The project started as a paper study, focusing on a block in the Golden Gate neighbourhood of Oakland. In 2020 a block in Fruitvale, at the southern end of the city, was selected to host a physical version of the EcoBlock project.[3]

[3] Z. Barr et al., *Accelerating the Deployment of Advanced Energy Communities: The Oakland EcoBlock* (Sacramento, CA: California Energy Commission, 2019); D.M. Kammen, 'Sustainable Design of Communities Dramatically Reduces Waste', *Scientific American*, 26 June 2017. Available at: http://bit.do/fJKjQ (accessed 20 December 2019). Renewable and Appropriate Energy Laboratory, *The Eco-Block project*, 2019. Available at: http://bit.do/fJKjR (accessed 26 March 2019); A. Salem, 'Cities of the Future: EcoBlock Project to Make Oakland Neighborhoods Emission Free', *UC Berkeley College of Environmental Design*, 2017. Available at: http://bit.do/fJKjV (accessed 20 December 2019).

GWL
Amsterdam, the Netherlands

PREVIOUS USE
Waterworks

CONSTRUCTION TIME
1995–1998

POPULATION
1,800

HOMES
600

AREA
6 hectares

→ A careful design of public space (■) creates a 'parochial' atmosphere in GWL's inner yards. The height of garden hedges is restricted;
neighbours can see each other when outside. It is a smart design
feature that sparks social interaction.

50 m

'It is about waking up to the sight of trees and the sounds of birds; neighbours that can become friends; kids that, at the age of three, can play outside unattended. And all this in the middle of a bustling, diverse city. Why do we not build more of this?'

Luca Bertolini
(long-time resident and professor of Urban Planning
at the University of Amsterdam)

Fig. 2.7 ↑ Aerial view of GWL.

A Lottery for Parking Spots — When you signed up to become a dweller of an apartment in the GWL neighbourhood (the former Municipal Waterworks terrain) in the early 1990s, chances of obtaining a parking permit were very slim (less than 20 percent). Abundant parking simply did not fit the concept of an eco-district where planning principles revolved around designing a sustainable mobility system, building a thriving public space, and using sustainable building materials. To distribute parking spaces among future residents, a lottery was organized. A handful of public housing associations funded the project in times where private investors were hesitant to invest. The latter felt the lack of parking spaces would hamper the interest of potential dwellers. The plan for GWL integrated historical buildings of this former water storage area, including a remarkable, monumental water tower, into the urban form. Aesthetically the newly built apartment blocks in the neighbourhood may come across as rather straightforward and not particularly awe-inspiring structures, but they include clever design interventions to spark social interaction. Think of shared hallways where residents meet and a restriction on the height of hedges so that gardens do not become isolated from the public space. The urban design enables a direct relationship with the outside environment, too: every apartment has either a garden, rooftop terrace, or sizable balcony, and about two-thirds of the neighbourhood is unpaved, to facilitate water drainage. The project used sustainably sourced, reused and reusable materials— sustainable pine wood for doors and stairs, reused concrete rubble, water-based paints. It helped limit the construction's environmental impact. GWL has become one of the most thriving and popular

Fig. 2.8 ↑ GWL's central boulevard is a pedestrian street.

Fig. 2.9 → One of GWL's monumental industrial buildings hosts a restaurant and several enterprises.

(4) City of Amsterdam, *Wonen in compacte Amsterdamse hoogbouw* (Amsterdam: City of Amsterdam, 2002); Except Integrated Sustainability, *Greenprint: Examples of Sustainable Practice in the Built Environment* (Rotterdam: Except Integrated Sustainability, 2011); N. Foletta and S. Field, *Europe's Vibrant New Low Car(bon) Communities* (New York, NY: Institute for Transportation & Development Policy, 2011); GWL, 'GWL Terrain: An Urban Eco Area', s.a. Available at: http://bit.do/fJKjY (accessed 20 December 2019); S. Melia, 'Carfree, Low-car—What's the Difference?', paper presented at the European Transport Conference, Glasgow, 11–13 October 2010; Stadsdeel Westerpark, *Eigentijdse ecologie: Gemeentewaterleidingterrein: Een autoluwe woonwijk in Amsterdam Westerpark* (Amsterdam: Stadsdeel Westerpark, 2000); J. Scheurer, *Urban Ecology, Innovations in Housing Policy and the Future of Cities: Towards Sustainability in Neighbourhood Communities* (Perth: Murdoch University, 2001), pp. 276–286; Stichting Ecoplan, *GWL-terrein* (Amsterdam: Stichting Ecoplan, 1997). Available at: http://bit.do/fJKjZ (accessed 20 December 2019).

neighbourhoods in Amsterdam. Cars are not allowed here. Small streets and alleys connect the neighbourhood with the surrounding urban fabric, providing access to nearby shops and parks. The lottery proved successful: only 6 percent of the transport trips made by GWL's residents are made by car. Talking about residents, they have been thoroughly involved in the operation of their neighbourhood since a community organization was founded in 1996. It has been safeguarding the original environmental ambitions of the place, communicating structurally and systematically about all things GWL, and as such contributing to the sense of ownership among residents.[4]

Hunziker Areal
Zurich, Switzerland

PREVIOUS USE
Concrete plant

CONSTRUCTION TIME
2012–2016

POPULATION
1,265

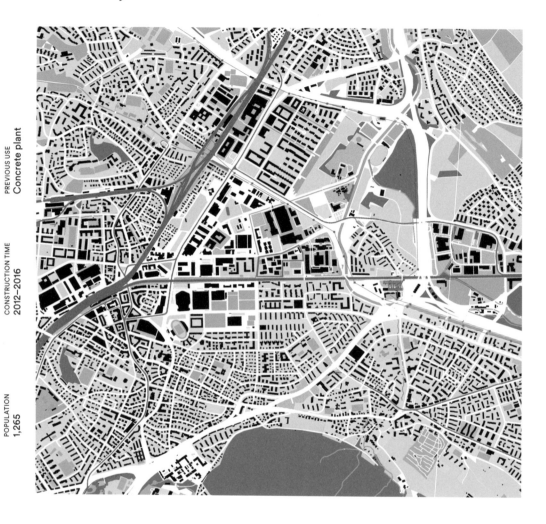

HOMES
373

AREA
5 hectares

→ A small parking garage and a few dedicated parking spots (ⓟ) here and there, that's all there is for Hunziker Areal's residents. Car ownership is severely restricted to people with disabilities or those who need a vehicle for work. Solar panels (■) cover many rooftops.

50 m

Fig. 2.10 ↑ Neighbourhood celebrations on Hunzikerplatz.

Fig. 2.11 → A playground at the southern end of the Dialogweg.

Fig. 2.12 (Next spread) Apartment in Haus A, designed by Duplex Architekten.

Elaborate Like a Swiss Army Knife — Residents of Hunziker Areal, at the northern edge of Zurich, need only 48 kWh of electricity for their daily needs: transportation, heating, goods. This is an impressive statistic: Swiss scientists have computed that global warming can be limited to two degrees if a 48 kWh power consumption limit per day is sustained worldwide. About <u>fifty housing cooperatives</u> joined hands in an overarching cooperative to build this small yet distinctive residential neighbourhood. In Hunziker Areal, owning a private car is only allowed for a very good reason, such as health or occupational needs—think of disabled people or taxi drivers. Public transit, cycling, and walking are the prevailing transport modes here; there are just about <u>fifty cars on a population of 1,200</u>, and driving amounts to a minor 6 percent of people's daily travel distance. Waste heat from a data server farm keeps dwellings warm. That largely suffices as compact building forms and <u>high-quality insulation</u> keep the demand for heating low. <u>Solar photovoltaics</u> generate 45 percent of household electricity consumption, which is fairly low anyway because of shared washing machines and freezers—which in turn reduce the living space that people require. Residents seeking to create their own sustainable initiatives are supported through common spaces and a <u>solidarity fund</u>. And it is not just the 'green elite' that resides in Hunziker Areal. The small apartments have <u>relatively low rents</u>, and some rents are subsidized through a system of interest-free loans from the government. Strict measures are in place to sustain social inclusivity: for about a fifth of the apartments there is a 17 percent discount on rent, and approximately 10 percent of the dwellings have been earmarked for disabled people, immigrants, and students.[5]

[5] Baugenossenschaft mehr als wohnen, *Fact Sheet: Baugenossenschaft mehr als wohnen*, 2017. Available at: http://bit.do/fJKj2 (accessed 20 December 2019); Baugenossenschaft mehr als wohnen, 'Wohnen die Richtigen in der Genossenschaft?', 2018. Available at: http://bit.do/fJKj3 (accessed 20 December 2019); 'Baugenossenschaft mehr als wohnen', *Wohnungsspiegel*, 2018. Available at: http://bit.do/fJKj4 (accessed 20 December 2019); Baugenossenschaft mehr als wohnen, 'Ein innovatives Bauprojekt', s.a. Available at: http://bit.do/fJKj6 (accessed 20 December 2019); Premio di Architettura Baffa Rivolta, 'Hunziker Areal: Housing cooperative mehr als wohnen', s.a. Available at: http://bit.do/fJKj9 (accessed 20 December 2019); U. Vogel, N. Nübold, and S. Schneider, *2000-Watt-Areale im Betrieb: Schlussbericht Pilotphase 2015/16* (Ittigen: EnergieSchweiz, 2017); World Habitat, *More than Housing*, 2017. Available at: http://bit.do/fJKkb (accessed 26 July 2019).

Kalasatama
Helsinki, Finland

PREVIOUS USE
Harbour and industrial area

CONSTRUCTION TIME
2009–2030s

POPULATION
25,000 (expected)

HOMES
Unspecified

AREA
175 hectares

↑ A neighbourhood as a test lab for apps for people to 'win' as much time as possible in a day, support community building, and reduce their environmental impact; fanning out from a subway station (●) that was completed in 2007, this is the 'smart' neighbourhood of Kalasatama.

A 25/7 Pilot for Smart Cities — Kalasatama is interesting for its objectives but controversial for its 'smart' strategy. Time is seen as scarce and valuable in Kalasatama, and so the key question for this neighbourhood is: how to waste as little time as possible? The main objective is to give people an extra hour of free time a day. To achieve this objective the neighbourhood is a living lab in which myriad smart apps are tested and evaluated. About a quarter of Kalasatama's residents participate in app experiments, as do a range of companies, policymakers, and researchers. Witrafi's Rent-a-Park is an apt example. It finds, books, and pays for parking spots for residents. There are also apps that support Kalasatama's social structure. KuntoKaverit connects elderly people with buddies who help them take an active part in the neighbourhood. Kotihiili assists residents in reducing their environmental impact by measuring their CO_2 emissions real-time and giving advice on sustainable behaviour. There are more tangible interventions for time-saving and social and environmental benefits, too. Smart energy infrastructure—combined with storage capacity—helps to find a balance between energy demand and supply. An underground, automated waste-collection system makes traffic-jamming, polluting garbage trucks redundant. Local services and amenities—a cinema, a centre for health and well-being, and a cultural centre— are clustered in buildings around the Kalasatama subway station, which opened its doors in 2007. They are easily accessible from all directions. Kalasatama illustrates the efforts to use 'smart' technology to create new sustainable neighbourhoods.[6]

(6) City of Helsinki, *Kalasatama: Culture and Life Close to the Heart of the City*, 2013. Available at: http://bit.do/fJKkc (accessed 20 December 2019); City of Helsinki, *Kalasatama: Life and Culture Next to Helsinki's City Centre*, 2018. Available at: http://bit.do/fJKke (accessed 20 December 2019); Helsinki Smart Region, *Agile Piloting in Kalasatama District Creates Urban Services with Users*, s.a. Available at: http://bit.do/fJKkg (accessed 20 December 2019); V. Mustonen, K. Spilling, and M. Bergström, *Cookbook: Recipes for Agile Pilots* (Helsinki: Forum Virium Helsinki/Smart Kalasatama, 2018). Available at: http://bit.do/fJ3ZX (accessed 20 December 2019); A. Pikkanen, *Kalasatama Smart City: This Smart City District Will Save People an Hour a Day*, 2017. Available at: http://bit.do/fJKkm (accessed 20 December 2019); Smart Kalasatama, *Hack into the Future: Helsinki's Kalasatama Providing one Blueprint for Tomorrow*, 2016. Available at: http://bit.do/fJKkp (accessed 20 December 2019).

Fig. 2.13 ↑ Brand new mid-rises and high-rises in Kalasatama.

Fig. 2.14 (Next spread) Sauna on the water, construction in the background.

Kronsberg
Hannover, Germany

PREVIOUS USE
Agricultural land

CONSTRUCTION TIME
1996–ongoing

POPULATION
7,300

HOMES
3,200

AREA
94 hectares

→ Kronsberg demonstrates a remarkable early attempt at building a layered sustainable structure (■), combining environmental and social agendas—high accessibility by public transport (—), plenty of nature-based solutions in the public space, a wide range of technical measures to reduce energy demand, and programmes aimed at community building.

Rainwater
retention area

Green public
space

Green public
space

KroKuS
neighbourhood
centre

Passive houses

Tram line

Green public
space

Rainwater
retention area

Green public
space

100 m

Fig. 2.15 ↑ The 'commons' in Kronsberg.

Multiple-tiered Sustainability Exhibited — Hannover organized the global exhibition Expo 2000, at the turn of the millennium. Kronsberg was built right next to the expo terrain to exhibit the state-of-the-art sustainable urban planning and simultaneously alleviate the city's housing shortage. The average distance from residences to tram stops is <u>only 350 metres</u>. The City of Hannover already owned most of the land and demanded high environmental standards for the new neighbourhood. A guiding principle was that <u>environmental and social issues</u> had to be approached in an integrated way. For instance, one project reduced residual waste production through a community-based approach, involving free advice and a neighbourhood network for repair and reuse. <u>Nature-based solutions</u> have also played an important role. Permeable surfaces and green roofs, as well as streams, ponds, trenches, and retention basins were integrated into the neighbourhood to drain rainwater naturally. These water features keep the environment cool in summer. Electricity savings, proper insulation, early passive-house projects, and co-generated district heating helped limit energy demand. And on-site solar panels and nearby wind turbines compensate the annual demand for electricity. In 2011, the annual average heating requirement for buildings was a low 45 kWh per square metre. KroKuS, a <u>neighbourhood centre</u>, has been offering cultural and creative space for all age groups in Kronsberg. KroKuS has been a meeting space ever since its doors opened for Expo 2000, when it was the hub for 'Kronsberg guides' who would organize neighbourhood contests, clean-up actions, and whatnot. Dedicated programmes have promoted the value of <u>diversity</u>. For instance, Habitat International Living welcomed migrants, and Fokus provided housing for the disabled. Some 85 percent of surveyed inhabitants indicated to be highly satisfied with their lives in Kronsberg in 2012. Their neighbourhood has received much praise for its early, serious, and ongoing attempt to be a model as a sustainable urban community.[7]

(7) City of Hannover, *Hannover Kronsberg Handbook: Planning and Realization* (Hannover: City of Hannover, 2004); City of Hannover, *Hannover-Kronsberg: 15 Jahre Erfahrung mit einem nachhaltigen Modellprojekt* (Hannover: City of Hannover, 2013); G.J. Coates, 'The City as Garden: A Study of the Sustainable Urban District of Kronsberg (Hannover), Germany', 47th International Making Cities Livable Conference, 10–14 May 2009, Portland, OR; H. Fraker, *The Hidden Potential of Sustainable Neighbourhoods: Lessons from Low-carbon Communities* (Washington, DC: Island Press, 2013); KUKA and City of Hannover, *Hannover Kronsberg: Model for a Sustainable New Urban Community* (Hannover: Kronsberg Environmental Liaison Agency [KUKA] and City of Hannover, 1998).

Merwede
Utrecht, the Netherlands

PREVIOUS USE
Warehouses and industrial area

CONSTRUCTION TIME
2022–2030s

POPULATION
12,000 (expected)

HOMES
6,000 (expected)

AREA
22 hectares

→ Two prerequisites for the development of Merwede are that it will not generate congested streets and will have a minor environmental footprint. So: fewer cars, more walking and cycling (—), and an alternative mobility plan altogether, with 'mobility hubs' (●) and several digital mobility services.

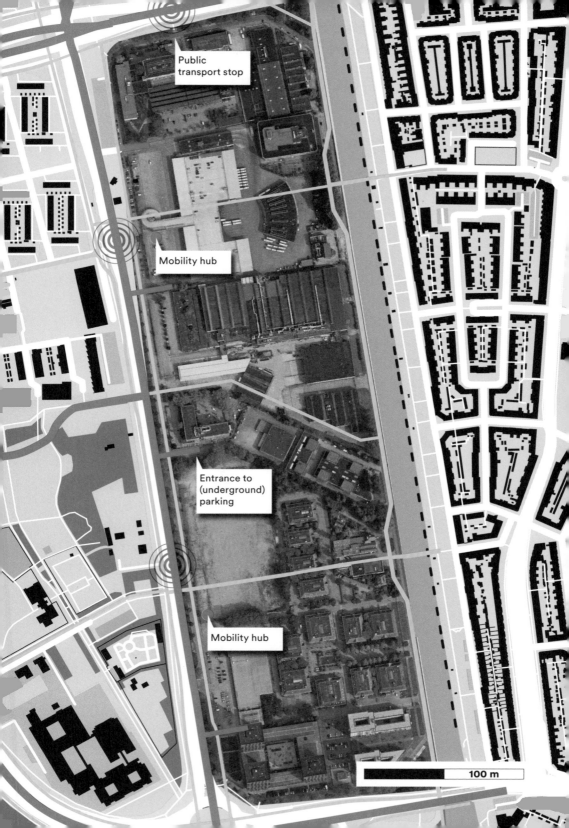

Public transport stop

Mobility hub

Entrance to (underground) parking

Mobility hub

100 m

'Proud of this new neighbourhood. Built for pedestrians and cyclists, energy-efficient and very green. I can't wait...'

Lot van Hooijdonk
(Councilor for Mobility and Energy, City of Utrecht)

Who Needs a Car Where Densities Are High and Algorithms Steer Mobility? — The image of 'healthy urban living' was once one of concrete high-rise buildings, spacious avenues for cars, and plenty of public green space. A functional city, oriented towards the automobile and characterized by clarity of design and a maximum of 'light, air, and space'. In today's Utrecht it implies something different: <u>active transport</u>—less cars, more walking and cycling—in combination with high densities and mixed use. The new masterplan for the neighbourhood Merwede aims at making this district a trailblazer for this kind of sustainable urban living. Close to Utrecht's old town, this new neighbourhood will host 12,000 residents on a piece of land of twenty-two hectares—a <u>remarkable density</u> in the Netherlands. Merwede has long remained an area of industry, large-scale retail and a bus and bicycle depot, but Utrecht's staggering housing demand has made redeveloping and repurposing the site inevitable. However, not without strict preconditions and limitations. Most peculiar is Merwede's <u>low parking norm</u> of 0.3 per housing unit. Building the envisioned 6,000 homes is only allowed if the traffic generated by the new neighbourhood will not become too much of a burden for the adjacent arterial

Fig. 2.16 ↑ Existing buildings in Merwede: Max and Lux et Pax.

Fig. 2.17 (Next spread) Rendering of Merwede: active transport and a variety of densities.

roads; there can only be room for 1,800 automobiles—both private and shared. In fact, driving within Merwede will be prohibited: cars have to be parked in one of the few (underground) car parks. A concept called 'parking at a distance' is launched to ensure the mobility of Merwedians: they are kindly requested to park their cars at a tram stop, a few kilometres away. Moreover, Merwede will host two 'mobility hubs' where residents can easily get access to shared cars or bicycles. These hubs consist of physical shops and a digital platform. While the City of Utrecht plays a critical role in developing the vision—it owns 35 percent of the land—much will depend on collaboration with commercial developers who own the remaining 65 percent of the land. Yet they too subscribe to the intention of this new neighbourhood for the future, focused on healthy urban living, provided they can agree on a viable business case.[8]

(8) Lot van Hooijdonk on Twitter, 9 January 2020. Available at: http://bit.do/ fJKkP (accessed 20 January 2020); Eigenarencollectief Merwede, *Voorlopig Ontwerp Stedenbouwkundig Plan Merwede* (Utrecht: Eigenarencollectief Merwede, 2020).

Nordhavn
Copenhagen, Denmark

PREVIOUS USE
Docklands

CONSTRUCTION TIME
2012–2040s

POPULATION
40,000 (expected)

HOMES
16,000 (expected)

AREA
200+ hectares

↑ The development of Nordhavn started at the southern end of a swath of industrial land and is planned to follow the path of a new rapid transit line.

Fig. 2.18 → A vast harbour area, up for redevelopment.

Fig. 2.19 ↑ Playground on the top of a parking garage in Nordhavn.

Living and Dwelling on Sustainable Islets — Like so many harbour cities,

after many decades of turning its back to the sea, Copenhagen has gradually opened up to the water, using the opportunities that water provides for housing and mixed-use development. Having started this move with the development of Sudhavn, the City of Copenhagen has now set its mind and actions to the development of Nordhavn, the northern part of the harbourside, where tens of thousands of people will come to work and live in the near future. Nordhavn is designed to have one job for every inhabitant. Canals will divide this urban delta into smaller islands and neighbourhoods, creating <u>urban diversity</u> and giving water an omnipresent role. The historic port identity

of Nordhavn is preserved by maintaining and retrofitting many of its existing structures and buildings. Nordhavn's islets will be connected by a 'green loop': a green route consisting of a pedestrian path and a cycling 'highway'. The stops of a corresponding rapid transit line will be located

Fig. 2.20 ↑ Swimming at the dock.
Fig. 2.21 (Next spread) Bicycles at the dock in Nordhavn.

within a few minutes' walking distance of every place in Nordhavn. It showcases an example of what is commonly referred to as 'value capturing': CPH City and Port Development (CCPD) provides and pays for the infrastructure upfront, but will largely recover those costs by collecting fees from owners of properties located close to transit stops. Finally, the City of Copenhagen—which has very ambitious climate targets overall—has also ensured the sustainability of Nordhavn's buildings by setting high and consistent energy targets, strict building codes, an obligatory connection to a climate-neutral low-temperature district heating network, and required approval by the CCPD of architectural designs. In Nordhavn, sustainability is not an explicit aim; it is considered a normal standard—ordinary, even.[9]

(9) M.C. Ariza, M.C. Quintero, and K.E. Alfaro, 'Integrated Urban Development: Copenhagen and Its Nordhavn Case', *Ciudades Sostenibles*, 14 June 2019. Blog of the Inter-American Development Bank. Available at: http://bit.do/fKdmv (accessed 15 October 2019); By & Havn, COBE Architects, Sleth Architects, Sangberg Architects, and Ramboll, *Nordhavn: Revision af strukturplanen fra 2009* (Copenhagen: By & Havn, 2018); CPH City and Port Development, *Nordhavnen: From Idea to Project: Inner Nordhavnen* (Copenhagen: CPH City and Port Development, 2012); J. Petersen and E. Heurkens, 'Implementing Energy Policies in Urban Development Projects: The Role of Public Planning Authorities in Denmark, Germany and the Netherlands', *Land Use Policy* 76 (2018), pp. 275–289.

Pearl District
Portland, Oregon, United States

PREVIOUS USE
Warehouses, light industry, railway yards

CONSTRUCTION TIME
1998–ongoing

POPULATION
17,250

HOMES
11,500

AREA
97 hectares

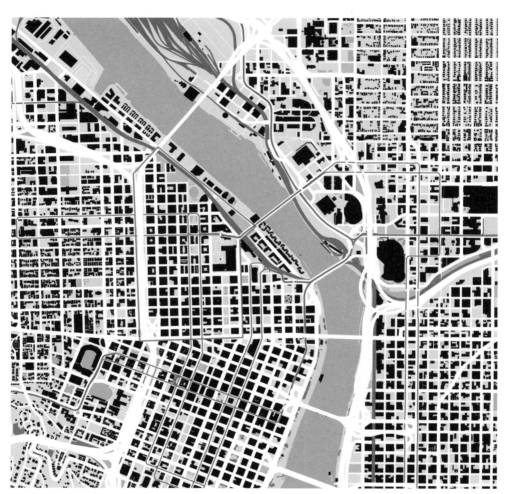

→ Different shades of red illustrate Pearl District's allowed density (■) in different areas within the neighbourhood, indicated by floor area ratio (FAR): the ratio of the gross floor area of buildings to the size of the land upon which they are built. The higher the allowed density, the darker the shade of red.

Fig. 2.22 ↑ Portland Streetcar in the Pearl District.

Fig. 2.23 ← Meetings on the corner.

The Neighbourhood is My Oyster —

Who else but the infamous urban planner Robert Moses helped design the transport system of Portland, Oregon, in the 1940s. The result was an extensive highway infrastructure, with arterial roads cutting right through the heart of the city. Add Portland's aged industry and an exodus to the suburbs, and the recipe for urban decline is obvious. However, the city managed to turn the tide. Most importantly, in the 1970s, the notoriously congested highway along the Willamette River, Harbour Drive, made way for a park. Pearl District appeared up north along the waterfront, right next to an Amtrak train station. Evolved somewhat gradually and being a slightly eccentric place today, 'Pearl' transformed into a vibrant district since the turn of the millennium. Many former industrial buildings were converted into offices, lofts and shops, creating a functionally mixed urban neighbourhood. Brand new apartment blocks were planted between

Fig. 2.24 ↑ Density in 'the Pearl'.

(10) Amtrak, *Northwest Train Routes*, 2019. Available at: http://bit.do/fJKkS (accessed 25 July 2019); City of Portland, *Pearl District Development Plan: A Future Vision for a Neighborhood in Transition* (Portland, OR: City of Portland, 2001). Available at: http://bit.do/fJKkW (accessed 20 December 2019); City of Portland, *North Pearl District Plan* (Portland, OR: City of Portland, 2008). Available at: http://bit.do/fJKk7 (accessed 20 December 2019); City of Portland, *Central City Plan District* (Portland, OR: City of Portland, 2019). Available at: http://bit.do/fJKk9 (accessed 20 December 2019); City of Portland, *Pearl District Access and Circulation Plan: Existing Conditions Report* (Portland, OR: City of Portland, 2012). Available at: http://bit.do/fJKmf (accessed 20 December 2019); Economic & Planning Systems, Inc., and Otak, *Final Report: City of Portland Central City Density Bonus and Entitlement Transfer Mechanism Update* (Portland, OR: City of Portland, 2015). Available at: http://bit.do/fJKmi (accessed 20 December 2019); Portland Development Commission, *River District Urban Renewal Plan* (Portland, OR: Portland Development Commission, 1998). Available at: http://bit.do/fJKmC (accessed 20 December 2019).

extant buildings. A cap was put on the neighbourhood's floor area ratio (FAR), limiting densities and thereby retaining a sense of human scale. Developers were granted permission to exceed this ceiling only if they developed prescribed types of (mixed) housing. Non-residential developments could achieve a 'FAR bonus' too, by adding sustainable features—such as green roofs and bike lockers. The neighbourhood's increased density and compact building plots helped limit travel times by foot, bicycle and public transport. Compared to the regional average, Pearl District residents, employers, and visitors travel half as much by car. Well over half of them go to work either on foot, bicycle, or by public transport, according to a 2008 survey.[10]

Strijp-S
Eindhoven, the Netherlands

PREVIOUS USE
Industrial park

CONSTRUCTION TIME
2002–2030s

POPULATION
1,700 (in 2020)

HOMES
4,000 (expected)

AREA
27 hectares

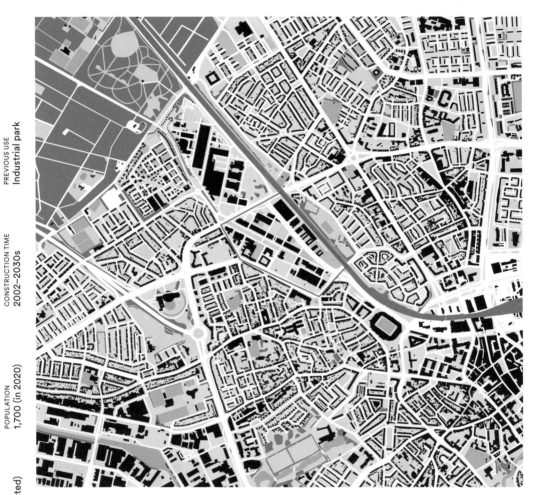

→ Once a 'forbidden city' that revolved around the production of light bulbs, Strijp-S now features car-free streets and a strategy that welcomes bars, restaurants, and shops in street plinths ( ) to stimulate a lively public space.

100 m

Fig. 2.25 ↑ Strijp-S hosts the Dutch Design Week every fall.

Fig. 2.26 (Next spread) The 'urban jungle' of Strijp-S.

Reviving a City's Rich History of Tech Innovation — There was a time that Philips Lighting designed and produced light bulbs. It happened at one of the key production sites of the corporation until the late-1990s:

Strijp-S, a 'forbidden city'. When Philips moved its headquarters to Amsterdam and many production sites were moved to other parts of the world, Eindhoven became somewhat of a post-industrial city. But times have changed; the city has again become a centre of innovation and industry, now with a key global role in the production of (machinery for) computer chips and the manufacturing of medical devices. Drawing on its industrial heritage buildings, Strijp-S is turning into a new neighbourhood to receive the incoming, high-educated workforce, to foster start-ups, and to welcome the creative industry. While skaters and hip hop collectives gather in well-preserved industrial buildings, former Philips employees are starting their own companies. The neighbourhood is being prepared for 5G and 6G networks. 'Smart' street lighting manages traffic flows: reducing lighting in residential areas helps limit nuisance during events, keeping visitors on designated routes. Data analysis and an app serve a continual optimization of the use of parking spots, and new technologies are applied to nullify the neighbourhood's gas consumption. The site is a testbed for a seasonal-heat storage system, using the site's contaminated groundwater, preventing it from spreading, and even accelerating the natural breakdown of the pollution. Strijp-S has become a success with its permanent experimenting and tinkering, conceptually, technologically, not to mention physically—its public space has been turned upside down three times since the start of the project. It will most probably gradually evolve into a more stable neighbourhood and ditto ecology.[11]

(11) Hydreco, 'Hydreco gaat Strijp-S voorzien van warmte en koude', press release 18 April 2018. Available at: http://bit.do/fJKm2 (accessed 20 December 2019); J.W. Kerssies, 'Strijp-S in Eindhoven ontwikkelt de leefbare stad van de toekomst', *Verkeer in Beeld*, 11 September 2018. Available at: http://bit.do/fJKm6 (accessed 20 December 2019); L. Roodbol and A. Mak, 'Strijp-S, Eindhoven: De -S van Strijp en Smart City'. *Gebiedsontwikkeling. nu*, 3 April 2014. Available at: http://bit.do/fJKm8 (accessed 20 December 2019); M. Theeuwen, 'Partijen maken afspraken over "betaalbaar" Strijp-S Eindhoven', *Eindhovens Dagblad*, 17 April 2018. Available at: http://bit.do/fJKm9 (accessed 20 December 2019).

Vauban
Freiburg, Germany

PREVIOUS USE
Barracks

CONSTRUCTION TIME
1998–2008

POPULATION
5,600

HOMES
2,000

AREA
41 hectares

Fewer Cars, Better Quality of Life — Vauban is well known as a thriving neighbourhood that has received international praise for its urban quality and approach to mobility. Vauban, a former military base on the outskirts of Freiburg, Germany, was predominantly redeveloped by _Baugruppen_, cooperatives of owner-occupiers, while commercial developers were given a far less prominent role. Its residents run the shops that are part of the cooperative, like the Quartiersladen at the corner of the Kurt-Tucholsky-Allee and the Vauban Allee. Nature reaches well into the neighbourhood as there are no hard barriers between the actual neighbourhood and its natural surroundings. The public domain at Vauban is relaxed, also because of the restrictions on car use. Drivers have to adapt to the speed of the other users, be they cyclists or pedestrians. In the main street the speed limit is thirty kilometres an hour. Consequently, the residential roads are used for all sorts of other activities: kids bring their soccer goals, adults gather tables and benches for get-togethers, and there are frequent flea markets. There is no parking space for cars in the streets, only for loading and unloading. Parking is restricted to car parks in the very corners of the neighbourhood, and is fully financed by car owners themselves. They pay up to 22,500 euros to purchase a spot. The blocks of the cooperatives have spacious communal rooms that are regularly used for meetings, birthday celebrations, movie nights, collective computer gaming, language courses for refugees, choir practice, yoga classes, card game tournaments, wine tastings, or joint lunches on days of shared garden work.[12]

(12) City of Freiburg, _Quartier Vauban_ (Freiburg: City of Freiburg, s.a). Available at: http://bit.do/fJKnn (accessed 20 December 2019); Except Integrated Sustainability, _Greenprint: Examples of Sustainable Practice in the Built Environment_ (Rotterdam: Except Integrated Sustainability, 2011); N. Foletta and S. Field, _Europe's Vibrant New Low-car(bon) Communities_ (New York, NY: Institute for Transportation & Development Policy, 2011); H. Fraker, _The Hidden Potential of Sustainable Neighbourhoods: Lessons from Low-carbon Communities_ (Washington, DC: Island Press, 2013); S. Melia, 'On the Road to Sustainability: Transport and Carfree Living in Freiburg', _Working Paper: UWE Bristol Healthy Cities Group_, 2006. Available at: http://bit.do/fJKnr (accessed 20 December 2019).

↑ Vauban shows no hard barriers with its natural surroundings and is marbled with a green public domain (■) for all sorts of social activities.

100 m

Fig. 2.27 ↑ Cyclists and pedestrians rule in Vauban.

Fig. 2.28 ← Tram line on the Vaubanallee.

'What makes living in Vauban so special for me, is not only the great location and the nice public spaces, which are perfectly designed for meeting, greeting, and chatting away, just where and whenever you run into somebody; more importantly, it is the do-it-yourself attitude of so many neighbours here, who organize for themselves what they want to see happening, like small flea markets and other activities. Yes, and perhaps the chickens that sometimes wander around the neighbourhood.'

Philipp Späth
(long-time resident and professor of Urban Environmental Governance at the University of Freiburg)

Villiers Island
Toronto, Canada

PREVIOUS USE
Harbour and industrial area

CONSTRUCTION TIME
2023–2040s

POPULATION
10,700 (expected)

HOMES
4,800 (expected)

AREA
22 hectares

→ Superimposed on the current situation in the Portlands, the plans for Villiers Island present a wide river valley (■) with extended parks (■) along its banks, thereby seriously mitigating flood risk in Toronto's Lower Don Lands.

100 m

Fig. 2.29 ↑ Construction worker bending steel in the Portlands.

Fig. 2.30 (Next spread) Aerial view of the current situation in the eastern section of Toronto's waterfront.

Room for Contestation: Who Decides on the New River Valley, How, and Where?

— Toronto is about to start yet another episode of rebuilding its vast 800-hectare waterfront. This time the most eastern section, the Portlands, is to undergo a bold transformation. In all of this, Villiers Island has long been regarded to become the new jewel in the crown, showing the latest ambitions with a neighbourhood for the future. The island will be an artificial creation: the mouth of the Don River currently makes a sharp right turn, incurring serious flood risk to the Lower Don Lands, thus inhibiting urban development. A new <u>wide river valley</u> with extended parks along its banks will manage water flows and buffer high water levels. But Villiers Island is more ambitious than merely offering a bold water management solution. It will simultaneously enable—physically and legally—the construction of a climate positive neighbourhood of almost 5,000 homes. Yet while the plans for its new layout had been almost fully worked out, for a while it became increasingly clear that the future of Villiers Island did not depend on the water engineering works; its future depended on the developments in Quayside, a nearby 5-hectare stretch of land just on the opposite side of the Keating Channel. Here Sidewalk Labs, a sister company of Google, sought to experiment with <u>new smart urban technologies</u>, a development that was regarded with suspicion by Torontonians. Not everyone seemed to appreciate that choices made in Quayside would logically affect the very development of the rest of the eastern docklands. Quayside was positioned to become a 'hub' for new infrastructure, adding a 'digital layer' to the future urban form. Here was a situation that unveiled the strategic role of Quayside: decisions taken on a site the size of a postage stamp were affecting developments down the line and along the Lake Ontario shoreline. And even though Sidewalk Labs pulled out of the project in the spring of 2020, technology will be a dominant force in the future of cities. <u>It is infusing everything, and it is probably unstoppable</u>. And so Villiers Island has been a crucial <u>site for urban contestation</u>, with effects that went way beyond the site, the Toronto Waterfront, and the Golden Horseshoe. It has been a site where choices are made about which urban future we want smart tech to facilitate.[13]

[13] City of Toronto, *Port Lands Energy Plan: Guidelines for a Net Zero District* (Toronto: City of Toronto, 2017). Available at: http://bit.do/fJKku (accessed 20 December 2019); City of Toronto and Waterfront Toronto, *Port Lands Planning Framework* (Toronto: City of Toronto and Waterfront Toronto, 2017); Waterfront Toronto, *Shaping the Future: Villiers Island Precinct Plan*, 2015. Available at: http://bit.do/fJKkw (accessed 20 December 2019); Waterfront Toronto, *Annual Report 2017/2018* (Toronto: Waterfront Toronto, 2018). Available at: http://bit.do/fJKkA (accessed 20 December 2019); Waterfront Toronto, *What Are We Building?*, 2019. Available at: http://bit.do/fJKkB (accessed 20 December 2019); Waterfront Toronto, City of Toronto, and Villiers Island precinct planning team, *Villiers Island Precinct Plan* (Toronto: Waterfront Toronto, 2017). Available at: http://bit.do/fJ4gD (accessed 20 December 2019).

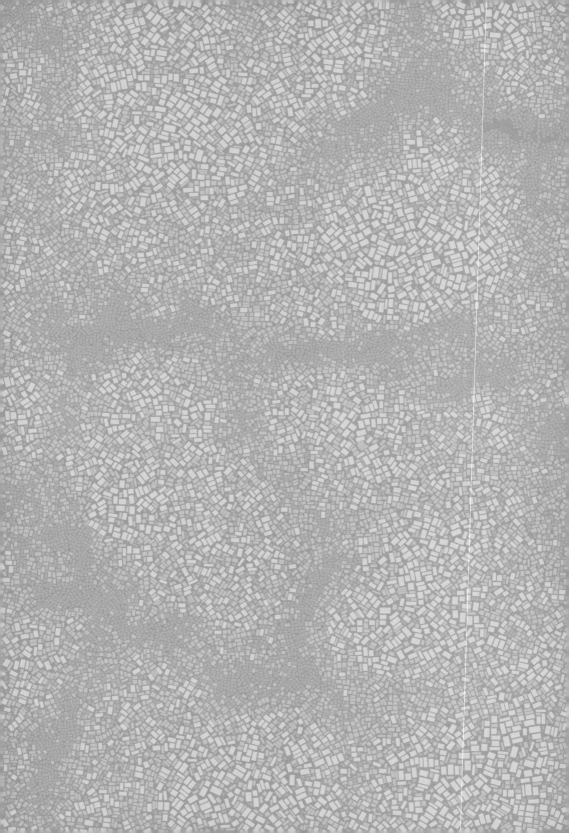

3 Analyzing Neighbourhoods for the Future

Fig. 3.1 Backyards in the northern section of Bo01.

Bo01
Malmö, Sweden

Fig. 3.2 Facts and figures on the development of Bo01

Area 20 hectares

....

Start date 1999

....

Date of completion 2011

....

Number of residents approx. 2,300

....

Project budget lack of unanimity about the costs[1]

....

Actors involved
— Bo01—City of Tomorrow AB (also known as Bo01 AB—
  special purpose entity for European Housing Expo)
— City of Malmö (lead developer; planner;
  funding provider for European Housing Expo)
— National Government of Sweden (funding provider for
  sustainability measures through Local Investment Program [LIP])
— Sydkraft—E.ON Sverige since 2005
  (developer; funding provider for European Housing Expo)
— European Union (funding provider for energy
  efficiency measures and project evaluations)
— Lund University, Malmö University, and National Energy Agency
  (researchers on energetic performance and other aspects)
— Architect-developer teams; less than twenty for the
  construction process toward the expo; well over twenty
  for the entire operation until 2011 (designers; developers)

[1] Jan-Erik Schütt, who was employed at Malmö's Department of Real Estate during the development of Bo01, mentions 485 million Swedish kroners as the total estimated cost before the expo. A 2005 economic analysis of Bo01—after several hundreds of homes had been built—reports a total cost of 510 million Swedish kroners versus a revenue of 405 million Swedish kroners. See: Schütt, 'Land Development Technology for Sustainable Development', 2013. See also: C. Anderstig and J. Nilson, *Bo Noll Ett: Samhällsekonomiskt Sett* (Stockholm and Malmö: Inregia, 2005).

Fig. 3.3 Timeline: key decisions and actions in the development of Bo01

Late 1980s	Kockums shipyard ceases production in Västra Hamnen
	Saab opens car factory in Västra Hamnen
1991	Saab closes car factory
1995	Visionary process on Malmö: Vision Malmö 2000
1996	City of Malmö is selected to organize European Housing Expo
	City of Malmö buys land in Västra Hamnen
1998	Foundation of expo organization: Bo01—City of Tomorrow AB
1999	City of Malmö publishes Quality Program, developed in collaboration with Sydkraft and developers
2000	Construction of Bo01 begins
2001	European Housing Expo (approx. 350 dwellings have been built)
2002–2011	Construction completed of remaining sections of Bo01 plan area

Bo01 – Depicting the City of Tomorrow in 2001

PREVIOUS USE
Shipyard

CONSTRUCTION TIME
1999–2011

POPULATION
2,300

HOMES
1,400

AREA
20 hectares

→ Green space () was one of the principles for the mosaic urban design of Bo01 and has come in different shapes and sizes, from large parks to shared patios, to achieve both climate adaptation and high-quality public space.

100 m

On 1 July 2000, Queen Margrethe II of Denmark and King Carl XVI Gustaf of Sweden opened the majestic Öresund Bridge connecting Denmark and Sweden. Overnight the cities of Copenhagen and Malmö became two halves of a new metropolis. Malmö contributed to the spirit of optimism by hosting a European Housing Expo in 2001. Its theme: 'City of Tomorrow'. The expo was held on the outer tip of a derelict shipyard district. The City of Malmö gave architect Klas Tham the freedom to design and build a new neighbourhood to express how we should imagine our cities of the future. His vision for the future was clear: the expo was to be about an ecological turn in urbanism.

The city of the twenty-first century was not for cars but for people, and to further this, a well-functioning neighbourhood had to become a showcase. Finding the city of the future should not just be a matter of looking for new technology; it is essentially also about recouping some of the wisdom of urbanism as it had developed before we reconstructed our cities to serve the automobile. The plot of the expo was known as 'Bo01': 'Bo' is the Swedish word for 'to live'; '01' is code for the first homes being delivered in the year 2001. At Bo01 some 1400 dwellings were developed between 2000 and 2011. Crossing the Öresund Bridge from Denmark to Sweden these days, either by car or express train, one can see Santiago Calatrava's Turning Torso, Bo01's signature building and a powerful symbol of Malmö's new urban confidence.

Bo01 has captured the imagination and is now a neighbourhood that marks Malmö's resurrection, still visited by urban planning delegations on an almost daily basis. They all want to learn how Malmö did it: developing a sustainable neighbourhood. Even after twenty years, Bo01 has important lessons to teach. In this chapter, we not only discuss its hallmark neighbourhood ecology, but also the neighbourhood arrangement that made it possible to incorporate climate mitigation, climate adaptation, and urban design long before it came into vogue.

Glimpses of a Rich Neighbourhood Ecology

How should we conceive of an urban neighbourhood if we take our social interaction and our ecological responsibility as starting points? Bo01, located in the former dockland of the Swedish city of Malmö looking out over the Öresund Strait towards Copenhagen, provides some answers. The neighbourhood is designed to maximize its performance in terms of energy conservation and renewable energy usage, explicitly addresses concerns over biodiversity, and goes a long way in managing water usage and water retention in innovative ways.

Sverige 12 Kr

Fig. 3.4 ↑ PostNord stamp depicting Bo01's Turning Torso.

Fig. 3.5 (Next spread) Sundspromenaden at the end of a summer's day.

In the winter, homes in Bo01 are heated by the heat of last summer. Ninety meters down, the limestone bedrock stores warm water and a heat pump extracts that water on request. Come summer, water stored in the winter keeps houses cool as sunny hours build up and temperatures rise. Solar energy provides extra heating and electricity, and any heating surpluses are transferred to other neighbourhoods through the city's district heating system—and vice versa, if the need arises.[1] A giant nearby wind turbine (Boel) was long used to generate electricity for Bo01. Boel has since been dismantled,[2] but now the Lillgrund Wind Farm off the coast of Malmö provides the electricity for more than 60,000 households.

For the urban design of the neighbourhood, the architects and urban designers harked back on design principles from before our cities were dominated by cars. The streetscape has a playful urban interior inspired by medieval villages: narrow alleys, intimate squares, lots of green spaces. No single structure or facade looks the same. There is no strict grid plan. Castle-like buildings on the outer edges of the neighbourhood shield the village from the cold winds. Intimacy, complexity, mystique, surprise: strolling Bo01 is observing urban design qualities that tend to evoke a sense of well-being. That is what Klas Tham, Bo01's chief architect, had in mind when spearheading the design process: a human scale that did not allow for cars to dominate the neighbourhood.

Bo01 can be cold and windy in winter. But in summer the neighbourhood is a popular destination for people from all over the city. When we visit on a warm and sunny day in the summer of 2019, it looks like the entire population of Malmö is gathering on Bo01's coastline promenade to hang out with family or friends → Fig. 3.5. Some people are from affluent areas, others come from disadvantaged communities scattered across the city. Bus 5 takes passengers directly from Rosengård, one of the poorest neighbourhoods of Malmö, to Bo01. The bus is packed and warm, and its passengers reveal the immigrant city that Malmö is, with communities originally coming from, for instance, the Balkans, Iraq, Poland, and Somalia. This touch of diversity enlivens street life. The boulevard as a heterotopia, a communal space for a segregated city,[3] adds to the infrastructures of conviviality that we observe in

[1] L. Lövehed, '100 Per Cent Local Renewable Energy', in *Sustainable City of Tomorrow: Bo01, Experiences of a Swedish Housing Exposition*, ed. B. Persson, pp. 100–105 (Stockholm: Formas, 2005).

[2] Utility company E.ON Sverige (an 'evolved' version of Sydkraft) removed the wind turbine in 2016, after the corporation had not been able to find spare parts to fix some maintenance issues. City hall refused to approve plans for a new, taller turbine on the same spot, as the far north-western end of the docklands had become a potential location for urban or industrial development.

[3] S. Gozal, 'Malmo, A Segregated City: Separating Fact from Fiction', *EUobserver*, 18 November 2019. Available at: http://bit.do/fJKmJ (accessed 19 November 2019).

Fig. 3.6 ↑ A busy summer's day on Bo01's waterfront.

Fig. 3.7 → The Kockums shipyard in its heyday, the 1960s and 1970s.

the multiplicity of smaller places for conversation and leisure—playgrounds, in-block shared gardens.

A Brief History of a Great Ambition

As much as Malmö's textile and shipyard industries had flourished in the mid-twentieth century, as dramatic was the city's downfall in the 1970s and 1980s. One of the city's major employers, the shipyard owned and operated by shipbuilding company Kockums, ceased its activities in the late 1980s. The Swedish national government stepped in to reboot activity in the area, granting car manufacturer Saab the opportunity to run a plant there, but that only helped for a year or two. Saab left in 1991. A 140-hectares stretch of abandoned, contaminated land remained, less than a kilometre from Malmö Central Station.

In 1994, Ilmar Reepalu was elected Malmö's mayor. He initiated a visionary process on the future of the city, which had lost its confidence and belief in better times. Vision Malmö 2000 culminated in two key aspirations to achieve Malmö's revival: establishing a university and organizing a housing expo. The city was to become a leading actor in the knowledge society, as the Vision Malmö 2000 stated.[4] The future of Malmö would revolve around the economy, business, and education. There was a fiscal agenda behind this, because the city was in dire need of money. Income tax is an important local revenue in the Swedish fiscal system, and Reepalu has always been open about his motivation to lure higher-income people to Malmö to increase its tax base. Many of them had left the city during Malmö's industrial heyday and had moved to villages outside the city proper. Now was the time to welcome them back to the city; to have them lift the city up again.

The imaginary of Malmö as a *sustainable* city did not take off until a couple of years later.[5] Public funds dedicated to sustainability measures became available and created a window of opportunity to define a theme for the housing expo that Vision Malmö 2000 had proposed. Ståle Holgersen and Andreas Malm, academic scholars and experts on Malmö's development, argued that environmental concerns evolved out of pragmatic reasons: '[T]he city responded to incentives on various scales and selected the most useful strategies on an ad hoc basis.'[6] A focus on sustainability and the environment evolved over the years, including designing and building Bo01 as a vehicle for this new imaginary. The European Housing Expo themed 'City of Tomorrow' generated the momentum and financial levers required.

The City of Malmö bought seventy hectares of land in the western section of Västra Hamnen—as the peninsular is called—in 1996.[7] Some twenty

[4] City of Malmö, *Vision 2000* (Malmö: City of Malmö, 1995).

[5] E. Dalman, 'From the Island to the Western Harbour: The Idea of Bo01 Is Born', in Persson, *Sustainable City of Tomorrow*, 2005.

[6] S. Holgersen and A. Malm, '"Green Fix" as Crisis Management: Or, in Which World Is Malmö the World's Greenest City?', *Geografiska Annaler: Series B, Human Geography* 97, no. 4 (2015), pp. 275–290. See also: E. Jönsson and S. Holgersen, 'Spectacular, Realisable and "Everyday"', *City* 21, no. 3-4 (2017), pp. 253–270.

[7] The municipality pre-emptively bought this stretch of land for 236 million Swedish kroner from an investment company owned the Wallenbergs, a prominent Swedish family. See: S. Holgersen, *The Rise (and Fall?) of Post-Industrial Malmö: Investigations of City-Crisis Dialectics* (Lund: Lund University, 2014), p. 32. See also: J.-E. Schütt, 'Land Development Technology for Sustainable Development', in *The Western Harbour: Experiences and Lessons Learned in Malmö, Sweden*, ed. B. Persson, pp. 65–71 (Malmö: Arkus, 2013).

hectares of this, on the very western tip, would become the exhibition space for the 2001 European Housing Expo. The tight deadline motivated city hall to accelerate its local planning processes. In 1998, the City advertised and sold development rights to several private property developers and obtained their commitment to participate in an association that would develop guidelines for building on the site—the Owners' Group, it was called.[8] It included the developers, the City of Malmö, and Bo01 AB. The latter was a temporary public company that was in charge of the planning and operation of the exhibition. On behalf of Bo01, AB, and the City of Malmö expo architect Klas Tham and then city architect Christer Larsson had the authority to approve every developer's choice of architect.[9] It was a high-paced and top-down-oriented operation: the expo deadline was approaching fast, so decisions were made frantically.

City hall approved the local plan for Bo01 in 1999,[10] after which the City of Malmö started allocating and selling plots to developers who had been involved in the Owners' Group. Construction did not start until spring 2000, and the expo opened its doors in spring 2001. At that point, about 350 housing units had been completed by tens of architect-developer teams who had worked on small-scale housing projects.[11] Just over 200,000 people would visit the event.

Malmö's story is now on everybody's lips. A city rising from its ashes like a phoenix, with Bo01 marking the moment of renaissance and take-off; the people we meet in Malmö know the metaphor all too well and gratefully use it. The storyline is compelling: a once-bustling blue-collar town finds itself in dramatic economic despair, makes a radical turn to a new sustainable imaginary, foregrounds itself on the world stage, and crawls out of a vicious circle. It is the storyline of a lost economy that reinvents itself and chooses a riveting new path.[12]

————Bo01 has matured as a neighbourhood, yet still is inspiring. It has a neighbourhood ecology that combines a sustainability profile with sociability. It offers an urban stage in the summer when everybody appreciates its beautiful location. The neighbourhood portrays one of the earliest attempts at ecological urbanism and therefore it deserves our attention. It is important to appreciate Bo01 as a child of its time: in the late 1990s, sustainable urban development was not nearly as high on the agenda as it has been since the late 2010s. As we present Bo01's neighbourhood arrangement, we disentangle how key actors managed to achieve the unlikely.————

[8] Urban Land Institute, *ULI Development Case Studies: Bo01*, 2004. Available at: http://bit.do/fJKmL (accessed 12 June 2019). See also: Persson, *The Western Harbour*, 2013.

[9] S. Anderberg, 'Western Harbor in Malmö', in *Reinventing Planning: Examples from the Profession*, ed. S. Nan, J. Reilly, and S. Klass, pp. 210–227 (The Hague: International Society of City and Regional Planners, 2015).

[10] B. Johansson, 'The Western Harbour from a Comprehensive Planning Perspective', in Persson, *The Western Harbour*, 2013.

[11] H. Fraker, *The Hidden Potential of Sustainable Neighbourhoods: Lessons from Low-carbon Communities* (Washington, DC: Island Press, 2013).

[12] Anderberg, 'Western Harbor in Malmö', 2015. See also: S. Holgersen, *The Rise (and Fall?) of Post-industrial Malmö: Investigations of City-crisis Dialectics* (Lund: Lund University, 2014). See also: D. Mukhtar-Landgren, *Planering för framsteg och gemenskap: om den kommunala utvecklingsplaneringens idémässiga förutsätttningar* (Lund: Lund University, 2012).

Pursuing Urban Quality

Fundamental to Bo01's praised look and feel has been the now-famous Quality Program which was designed in five months by the Owners' Group.[13] It was a holistic set of guiding principles and standards for building a new, unique Malmö neighbourhood that would revolve around renewable energy, biodiversity, and water. There was no trade-off: urban design qualities went hand-in-hand with quantitative standards and measures for environmental sustainability. Klas Tham's early sketches of Bo01 indicated that pedestrians and cyclists would rule the streetscape; a wealth of vegetation would adorn both public space and the interior; and water would be visible from every single housing unit. The parallel to Malmö's medieval town plan was obvious, even for laypersons.→ Fig. 3.8

The Quality Program was imposed on every single development contract that was signed on the expo site so as to harness the human scale and a wide range of ecological and energetic objectives. It contained Klas Tham's masterplan, as well as an allocation of responsibilities among members of the Owners' Group. It was the core steering instrument for the development of the neighbourhood: architectural quality, choice of material, energy consumption—all of it was included in a comprehensive agenda for not just sustainability, but also high-quality design, technology, and information services.[14] The abstractions of the masterplan trickled down to sets of 'agreed basic standards' under seven categories: public space; green spaces; technical systems and infrastructure; social life; buildings; in-home qualities; and courtyards and forecourts. It was a sheer endless list of both strict and loose constraints, from plot sizes and building heights to vistas and visuals.

The workings of the Quality Program became especially clear in how biodiversity was prioritized and planned for. Gardens had to serve as habitats. Ponds, canals, parks, and trees had to be everywhere. The green plan for Bo01 was about creating micro-versions of wetlands, and the openly natural environment was to facilitate stormwater runoff like no sewage system could. Annika Kruuse still takes pride in how she managed to coordinate a generic system of factors and points that made biodiversity so prominent in the Bo01 development. We meet her on her last day as a public official at the City of Malmö. Each proposed project for Bo01 had to score at least 10 out of 35 'green points' to be granted permission.[15] Gardens were to be home to a variety of species, both plants and animals, so developers were forced to think of bird boxes, soil depths, frog habitats, indigenous herbs, and wildflowers. 'It is the first time the developers have discussed marketing properties according to green criteria', said project manager Eva Dalman in The Guardian in 2009.[16] Additionally, a 'green space factor' was designed to guarantee a minimum amount of

[13] Bo01 Framtidsstaden, Quality Programme Bo01: 1999-03-31 (Malmö: Bo01 Framtidsstaden, 1999). See also: B. Persson and E. Dalman, 'Investing in Sustainable Urban Development', in Persson, Sustainable City of Tomorrow, 2005.

[14] A.M. Madureira, 'Physical Planning in Entrepreneurial Urban Governance: Experiences from the Bo01 and Brunnshög Projects, Sweden', European Planning Studies 22, no. 11 (2014), pp. 2369–2388.

[15] Bo01 Framtidsstaden, Gröna Punkter (Malmö: Bo01 Framtidsstaden, 1999).

[16] C. Fry, 'Wanted: Natural Residents to Share Up-and-Coming Urban Quarter', The Guardian, 2 January 2009. Available at: http://bit.do/fJKmM (accessed 12 June 2019). See also: City of Malmö, Green Plan for Malmö 2003: Summary (Malmö: City of Malmö, 2003).

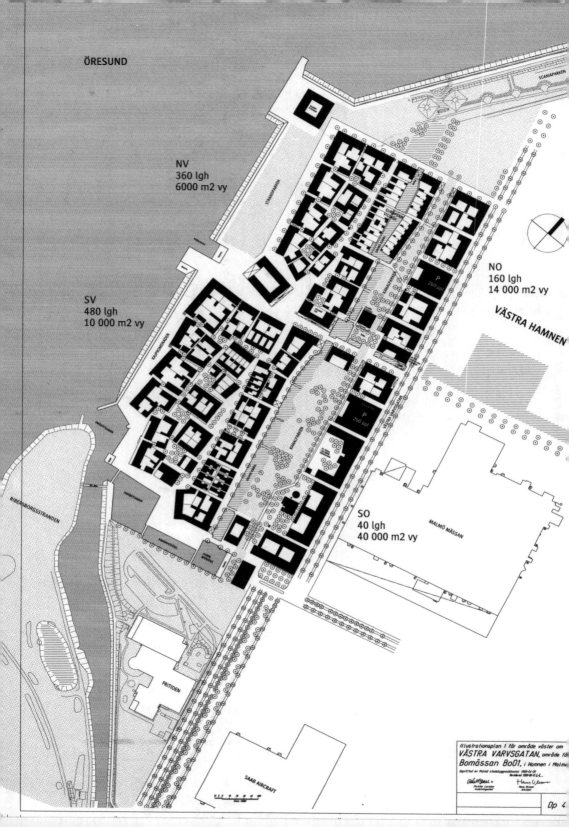

ÖRESUND

NV
360 lgh
6000 m2 vy

SV
480 lgh
10 000 m2 vy

NO
160 lgh
14 000 m2 vy

VÄSTRA HAMNEN

SO
40 lgh
40 000 m2 vy

MALMÖ MÄSSAN

RIBERSBORGSSTRANDEN

FRITIDEN

SAAB AIRCRAFT

SCANIAPARKEN

Illustrationsplan 1 för område väster om
VÄSTRA VARVSGATAN, område för
Bomässan Bo01, i Hamnen i Malmö

Dp 4

green space per building plot.[17] The more heavily a developer chose to exploit a plot, the greater the demands for compensation would be.

The Quality Program presented the bottom line of Tham's conviction: shifting to sustainable societies requires alternatives that are not just rationally sound, but prove more attractive to people than today's unsustainable societies. Sustainable neighbourhoods need to show the world that 'green' comes with comfort, pleasure, excitement, and beauty. By expressing a common aim and prescribing minimum levels of quality, a norm was set.[18] The output specifications lacked hard incentives, though—bonus mechanisms, sanctions, penalties. And so the Quality Program was a recommendation rather than a mandatory requirement. Mikael Edelstam, an environmental consultant who co-authored the Quality Program as Bo01 AB's head of environment, expresses how he would have loved to include sanctions in the arrangement for Bo01. 'It was a lesson I took from Hammarby Sjöstad in Stockholm, that you need to have hard sanction opportunities.' But instead, it was decided to take a more informal route: 'If they would not perform up to the standard that they promised, they would have a harder time getting a deal with the city next time.'

Public Money Talks

'Nobody wanted to build there.' Per-Arne Nilsson, Malmö's environment chief, cuts to the chase when we discuss Bo01 in his office. The Quality Program did not discuss financial aspects, and there was no obvious funding mechanism for Bo01. To pull off an initiative of this kind and also generate the interest of private-sector developers was all but plain sailing. There was no precedent; there was no evidence of there being a viable business case in the realm of building radically sustainable neighbourhoods.

Nilsson started working at Malmö's Department of Environment in the late 1980s and still works from the red-brick building on Bergsgatan 17, just south of the historic city centre. He remembers how the city had to come up with some incentives for developers. He and his colleagues would approach them and say: 'If you do this now and do something good, we could give you good plots later on.' They had to pull some tricks to get the developers on board because a business case was lacking. There were no precedents to fall back on when it came to green building at this scale and with these strong ties to high-quality urban design. To add to the complexity, Malmö's housing market was rather slow at the time. Developers were anxious about the limited demand for housing and imminent vacancies, so they had their reservations about the plan. Bo01 hardly allowed for economies of scale as the Quality Program almost exclusively prescribed small-scale plot development. Moreover, as the City of Malmö owned the land, it had considerable power to impose things on developers.[19]

Fig. 3.8 ← Map of Bo01 from the Malmö City Planning Office.

[17] Bo01 Framtidsstaden and City of Malmö, *Grönytefaktor för Bo01* (Malmö: Bo01 Framtidsstaden, 1999).

[18] E. Dalman, *Western Harbour: Sustainable Urban Development in Malmö*, 2008. Available at: http://bit.do/fJKmR (accessed 12 June 2019).

[19] J. Fitzgerald, *US Planners Can Learn Lessons from the Successes of Malmö's Eco-districts*, 2016. Available at: http://bit.do/fJKmT (accessed 12 June 2019).

While this condition eventually enabled the crafting of a Quality Program in the first place—and the worthy commitments on the part of developers it included—getting it done required hard and savvy work.

Two levers ultimately helped the plan come together and make it feasible. First, the foundation and workings of Bo01 AB proved pivotal. As a special purpose vehicle with a key role in planning and operating the expo, Bo01 AB was an area-based agency that could draw upon creative powers and ideas, overshadowing Malmö's daily planning routines while remaining able to develop legit plans.[20] Environmental consultant Mikael Edelstam emphasizes how the speciality of this situation created an opportunity to raise bars: 'A special purpose vehicle for delivering something extra is key…. I think this breaking out of normal boundaries is key to getting something really different done.' The expo was a perfect excuse for city planners to go out on a limb and find ways to build confidence among prospective developers so that they would embark on the catalyst platform that Bo01 was to become, with the foundation and operation of the Owners' group an example. Early involvement of developers alleviated their sense of risk, and Malmö's then head of City Planning Department, Mats Olsson, had an extensive network in the real estate sector, which helped in pulling some strings. Planning scholar Mafalda Madureira puts it aptly in her account of the planning process for Bo01: the creation of Bo01 AB 'allowed informal procedures and networks to be developed parallel to the action of the planning department'.[21] Informal meetings under the umbrella of the special purpose vehicle were vital in bringing developers in, helping them to shift their loyalties toward Bo01 AB.

The second lever was arguably more important than the expo-aroused sensation and planning processes: it was public investment. In the late 1990s, Per-Arne Nilsson and his colleagues successfully applied for national government subsidies earmarked for sustainability activities. This Local Investment Program (LIP) funding, as it was called, amounted to 250 million Swedish kroner (some 24 million euros).[22] Earlier that decade, Nilsson had already collected a couple of millions for the remediation of contaminated land at the Bo01 project site, but that had not nearly been sufficient to operate a business case for a sustainability programme as comprehensive as Bo01's. The bottleneck was in negotiations with Sydkraft, a Malmö-based power company, about developing a highly innovative energy system that would be fully based on local renewable energy. Sydkraft's engineers and financial specialists felt uncomfortable doing this entirely at their own expense. Mikael Edelstam, as he recollects his experience as a Bo01 insider: 'This was a core investment for them, in a high-profile area, and there was technical and commercial risk…. So, by applying for external funding, we thought we might pull them along, with the carrot instead of the stick.'

[20] Madureira, 'Physical Planning in Entrepreneurial Urban Governance', 2014.

[21] Ibid.

[22] For a project to be eligible for LIP funding, it had to aspire to a wide range of sustainability goals, such as reducing environmental impact, enhancing energy efficiency, increasing reuse and recycling, and preserving and strengthening biodiversity. See: D. Nilsson, 'The LIP Programme: A Prerequisite for the Environmental Initiatives', in Persson, *Sustainable City of Tomorrow*, 2005, p. 11.

The Bo01 team also successfully applied for European Union funding amounting to 1.5 million euros to spend on the energy concept. Malmö's former head of the city's Sustainable Development Unit and now consultant, Trevor Graham, argues that without that money it would have been very difficult for Richard Bengtsson, the then CEO of Sydkraft's district heating subsidiary, to make the case for a wildly progressive energy system before his board. The utility company was sticking its neck out: it sought solutions that could open new markets and business opportunities, but as with all risky endeavours, it could also all fall apart.[23]

————The coming together of generic rules for high quality and generous public resources for adventurous energy solutions was fundamental to realizing Bo01. It became the first neighbourhood in the world that could make the claim of being carbon neutral and able to prove this with data on its metabolism—its flows of materials and energy.[24] But as for most first attempts, Bo01's shot at ecological urbanism also came with limitations and missed opportunities. We can learn a lot from how actors did it, yet even more from the mistakes that were made and to what extent lessons learned have travelled.————

Learning from an Exemplar #1: A Rebound Effect

Though a poster child for constructing sustainable neighbourhoods worldwide, Bo01 also shows how difficult the relationship between a sustainable home and a sustainable lifestyle can be. Although Bo01's energy system is still operating on renewable resources, many buildings consume significantly more energy than the models foresaw.[25] The gap largely has to do with the residents and how they live their lives at home. Mattias Örtenvik, based at E.ON Sverige headquarters and head of the company's Sustainable City branch, explains it allegorically to us: 'We always say that LED televisions are a lot more energy-efficient, but that is correct in only one case: when you have just one television and it has a 28-inch screen.... We tend to forget that.' It is a 'rebound effect': energy savings are often cancelled out as people tend to use the money saved for new consumption. In the end, the residents of Bo01, while living in an emblematic sustainable neighbourhood, have increased their energy consumption over the past two decades. The tagline of Bo01 has always been that sustainable living should be effortless, but the irony is that it perhaps delivered a little too well on this. Li Lövehed, an engineer who was involved in the development of the energy concept for the neighbourhood, confesses that it would have made sense to exert more effort on the consumer side in the earlier phases of the project—for instance by involving (future) residents more or differently.[26]

[23] T. Graham, 'The Birth of a New Urban Governance', in Persson, *The Western Harbour*, 2013, pp. 72–78.

[24] H. Fraker, *The Hidden Potential of Sustainable Neighbourhoods: Lessons from Low-carbon Communities* (Washington, DC: Island Press, 2013).

[25] A. Nilsson and A. Elmroth, 'The Buildings Consume More Energy than Expected', in Persson, *Sustainable City of Tomorrow*, 2005, pp. 107–113. See also: C. Rolén, 'Environmental Assessment: A Complicated Task', in Persson, *Sustainable City of Tomorrow*, 2005, pp. 53–60.

[26] L. Lövehed and R. Bengtsson, 'One Hundred Percent Renewable Energy Production at Bo01', in Persson, *The Western Harbour*, 2013, pp. 128–132.

The gap between the sky-high sustainability ambitions of the late 1990s and how residents live in Bo01 today is not visible to the naked eye. But Malmö's city planners are the first to admit that the energy consumption in the neighbourhood has been off the mark and higher than anticipated. Increased screen time in households has not been the only culprit, though. Insulation values of wall and roof assemblies, the size and orientation of windows, monitoring and controlling heating systems, roof pitches, airtightness, and thermal bridging; there is no doubt that meticulously designing to low energy demands required shifts in thinking and engineering on the part of architects back in the late 1990s. They were new to these themes or new to the quite holistic approach that the Quality Program involved; they had been selected for this job based on their track record of good architecture, not their energy awareness.[27] Developers had hardly ever thought about the environmental impact of building materials, or sustainability solutions at the plot level, in combination with high-quality architecture and design. Modelling energy demand was in its infancy, as was the environmental assessment of buildings.[28] And the development of renewable energy resources was probably higher on the agenda than the construction of energy-efficient buildings.[29]

'The construction sector did not yet seem ready to work systematically on environmental construction.'[30] And of course, Bo01's planning and construction processes required hasty decision making because of the daunting deadline of the expo. Li Lövehed admits that the placement of solar collectors and cells could have been better. Figures on the 2002 and 2003 energy production indicated that collectors produced a meagre 60 percent of their projected kilowatt hours.[31]

Miscalculations and misrepresentations were omnipresent, but the impediments of all this pioneering work became clear only after the fact. When consultant Mikael Edelstam talks about the energy calculation tools used, he addresses how developers and architects forgot to include incoming sun rays and the cooling that would be needed when you have large windows. But the summer season comes with many hours of sun. Large windows are everywhere in Bo01, so in many homes the temperature rises drastically when the sun is shining. Cooling systems consumed more energy than anticipated, and at some point, residents started buying air conditioners. The story can be told the other way around, too: large glazed sections along the promenade are under serious wind and rain pressures, which triggers excessive energy consumption patterns. The only quantitative requirement that was included in the Quality Program, an annual energy demand for each home of 105 kilowatt-hours per square meter, evaporated.

[27] Nilsson and Elmroth, 'The Buildings Consume More Energy than Expected', 2005.

[28] B. Larsson and U. Wallström, 'Quality Programmes: An Aid to Sustainable Building', in Persson, Sustainable City of Tomorrow, 2005, pp. 41–50. See also: Rolén, 'Environmental Assessment', 2005.

[29] G.D. Austin, 'Case Study and Sustainability Assessment of Bo01, Malmö, Sweden', Journal of Green Building 8, no. 3 (2013), pp. 34–50.

[30] P.-A. Nilsson, C. Rolén, and R. Zinkernagel, 'From Environmental Evaluation of Buildings to Sustainability Certification of Districts', in Persson, The Western Harbour, 2013, pp. 110–118.

[31] Lövehed and Bengtsson, 'One Hundred Percent Renewable Energy Production at Bo01', 2013.

Learning from an Exemplar #2: The Human Scale

Cars were hardly anywhere to be seen in Bo01's early days. But when we explore the neighbourhood on foot on a bright day in February 2019, we stumble upon a gigantic multi-storey car park, just next to the Turning Torso. Cars have crept in over the years, so it seems. From the look of it, the automobile has become the default transport mode elsewhere in Västra Hamnen, the shipyard-turned-sustainable city that encompasses Bo01 and several other neighbourhoods.[32] As we explore the sustainable city by bike, we observe the differences between Bo01 and other areas of the peninsula. We come to appreciate how Bo01 stands out. Finishes look more conventional or sober in adjacent areas. Blocks are undeniably larger. Avenues become wider and cars are everywhere. We come across four more multi-storey car parks, not to mention a gigantic shopping mall on the eastern end of Bo01's wetlands. It contrasts with the human scale of Bo01 that impressed us so much.

The urban morphology of Bo01 still stands. The human scale of the urban design remains probably its most important asset: the small-scale street pattern, the equally small scale and diversity of the built structures, and the serenity of its wetlands, parks, alleys, and boulevards → Fig. 3.9. But from the look of it, this approach to the urban fabric did not hold up in successive developments in Västra Hamnen, an area that has been advertised as a world-leading attempt to building and dwelling sustainably too.

'The challenge that has been experienced ever since is replicating that human scale. And one of the issues associated with it is cost.' Trevor Graham explains that the pressure on keeping down costs became a key element for everyone involved in Västra Hamnen. It implied higher volumes and more floor space. The contrast with Bo01 is stark, he says:

The advantage of Bo01 was that there was a deadline.... And this is the showcase to the world, so at that point you've got to pull out all the stops to get there. So, everything is possible. That was kind of the spirit of that development at that point in time.

Fig. 3.9 (Next spread) Bo01's diverse urban design from above.

[32] The modal split in Western Harbour in 2013 was as follows: car trips—thirty percent; public transport trips—twenty-five percent; bicycle trips—twenty-five percent; walking trips—seventeen percent; and other trips—three percent. See: T. Koglin, 'Urban Mobilities and Materialities: A Critical Reflection of 'Sustainable' Urban Development', *Applied Mobilities* 2, no. 1 (2017), pp. 32–49. See also: City of Malmö, *Resvaneundersökning i Malmö 2013* (Malmö: City of Malmö, 2014).

[33] B. Persson and G. Rosberg, 'A Book About the Western Harbour', in Persson, *The Western Harbour*, 2013, pp. 13–16.

When Graham talks about what happened when the expo's doors closed, he addresses how planners were pulled back into the harsh realities of business as usual: economic drivers, political drivers, no sharp deadline. Bo01 AB went bankrupt, and Malmö's City Planning Department took it over for the next chapters of the former shipyard's revival. It became harder to make rigorous, bold decisions, also because some large stretches of land were owned by private-sector developers.[33] The question of how to achieve the human scale of Bo01 *at* scale remained unanswered, almost unaddressed. When you walk through

Västra Hamnen you can almost literally see the train of thoughts that planners and developers followed while crafting Bo01's successors, like Flagghusen and Fullriggaren (code names: Bo02 and Bo03), or Dockan and Masthusen. There has been a variation in ambitions toward sustainability across Västra Hamnen, especially in relation to cost efficiency, and as a result, urban form. A market for sustainable urban development has evolved, but business cases continue to thrive on scale unless significant public investments are provided. 'Value-based planning' has been the agenda on privately-owned lots like Dockan, says landscape architect Bengt Persson,[34] and has led to a rather monotonous, grand urban landscape—over-dimensioned roads and plazas, 'a large-scale sensation'.[35]

The human scale, a crucial part of Bo01's planning concept, never made a comeback in Malmö on a scale and structure akin to the neighbourhood. Bo01's comprehensive urban design is unparalleled, even twenty years after the fact.

Malmö and the Future: For Everyone?

Bo01 has become an exemplar. It shows the world that sustainable solutions in urban development are achievable without undermining the comfort many of us are used to. It also demonstrates that it can be done in an urban layout that is both convenient and functional as an enabler of human interaction that reaches far beyond one or two blocks. Bo01 has been a 'flywheel', too. No one had foreseen Malmö to become this cutting edge in sustainable urban development—not after the local shipbuilding industry had taken hit after hit, unemployment and crime afflicted communities all over town, and the city was on its knees in the mid-1980s. The downfall had included an astounding loss of 35,000 jobs.[36] 'To new beginnings' is what the European Housing Expo implied, and the resources that came with it allowed for unseen solutions. Bo01 has been a bold try-out that truly makes the delicate connection and goes beyond technique and technology. That is what makes this neighbourhood in Malmö so different from many other places.

The story of Bo01 depicts experiences that are vital to take on as lessons for neighbourhoods for the future elsewhere. The learnings have taken the shape of recurring dilemmas, though. The green paradox endures and the human scale remains a difficult trait to achieve. And yet Malmö probably faces bigger challenges on its way to becoming a thriving, sustainable city. The elephant in the room is the series of persistent socioeconomic challenges in disadvantaged neighbourhoods. The distance between the 'eco glamour' of Bo01 and crime-infested neighbourhoods is small in kilometres but unpleasantly large in figurative terms. Malmö is a Janus-faced city indeed: its image of sustainability, of being a booming town both culturally and economically, is at odds with unemployment and poverty rates in several neighbourhoods and with the income disparity in general.[37]

[34] B. Persson, 'Urban Planning in the Western Harbour', in Persson, *The Western Harbour*, 2013, pp. 24–25.

[35] T. Hellquist, 'Structure, Space and Design in the Western Harbour', in Persson, *The Western Harbour*, 2013, pp. 26–32.

[36] M. Olsson, 'Bo01 as a Strategic Project', in Persson, *Sustainable City of Tomorrow*, 2005, p. 9.

[37] J. Lenhart et al., 'Cities as Learning Organisations in Climate Policy: The Case of Malmö', *International Journal of Urban Sustainable Development* 6, no. 1 (2014), pp. 89–106.

Bo01's boulevard along the Öresund Strait is there for everyone to parade and play, but the neighbourhood has not become a place for everyone to live in. It is popular among—and affordable for—middle-income and upper-middle-income groups. Mikael Edelstam points out a classic critique of Bo01 and Västra Hamnen in general: 'It would have been good to show that a sustainable, well-designed, attractive neighbourhood could also be for the larger part of the citizens.' Bo01 has missed the opportunity of also becoming an inclusive community. Trevor Graham, who has almost three decades of experience in building sustainable communities—often in disadvantaged neighbourhoods—revisits the rhetoric in the city and the media at the time: 'It was being seen as housing for the rich, in a city that was on its knees. So there were, you know, lots of socioeconomic problems. And here we were building a ghetto for rich people. A gated community.' Bo01, and Västra Hamnen as a whole, have had to deal with this image to this very day. Affordable housing has appeared on the agenda, but it still is generally too expensive for low-income families to live on the peninsula, says Christer Larsson, Malmö's director of city planning, when we visit him in his office in *Stadshus*. The neighbourhood does house some people on quite varied incomes with varied backgrounds, but it is hard to deny that the socioeconomic disparity within the city persists. While Malmö's finances have eased, the trickle-down benefits that were hoped for in the development doctrine of the 1990s have not come about.

Yet in the aftermath of Bo01, a focus on energetic sustainability has prevailed and evolved in Malmö. City planners collaborated with developers, builders, and architects in the 'ByggaBoDialogen' (Building-living dialogue) to, for instance, improve energy efficiency standards and reduce production costs for the next planning endeavours in Västra Hamnen.[38] Planners took developers to Bo01's best-performing buildings to lay out the lessons learned. The cities of Malmö and Lund together designed a programme aimed at supporting and facilitating sustainable construction, the Environmental Building Programme. It offers a classification system for buildings and sets requirements that go beyond national building standards.[39] Then there is the use by default of other environmental certification systems for single buildings, as well as blocks and districts—the likes of BREEAM, GreenBuilding, LEED, and Nordic Swan. Västra Hamnen continues to be a welcome testbed for new techniques that can be applied elsewhere afterwards with less hesitation and uncertainty.

Now there is a business case for sustainable building, and Malmö's latest urban expansion, Hyllie, reflects very well how energy efficiency standards have become part and parcel of city building. As the leading 'climate-smart city district' in the Öresund Region, this neighbourhood will provide about 10,000 homes and 10,000 offices with renewable or

[38] City of Malmo and ISU, *Malmö: Making Sustainability Reality* (Malmö: City of Malmö and Institute for Sustainable Urban Development, 2008). See also: J. Fitzgerald and J. Lenhart, 'Eco-districts: Can They Accelerate Urban Climate Planning?', *Environment and Planning C: Government and Policy* 34, no. 2 (2016), pp. 364–380.

[39] Lenhart et al., 'Cities as Learning Organisations in Climate Policy', 2014.

recycled energy, following the signing of a 'climate contract' in 2011. In this contract, the City of Malmö, E.ON, and VA SYD (a public water utility) made arrangements to become a global benchmark for sustainable urban development. Indeed, today's practice of sustainable development is one of contracts—clear definitions and accountability lines.

Sustainable building has become the *modus operandi* in Malmö. But perhaps it has also tipped the scales toward 'kilowatt-hours', leaving behind the elegant and wise craft of neighbourhood building that we aspire to put on the agenda with this book. The results become predictable; it is easier to create the image of a sustainable city than to create life.

DISCOURSE	— Malmö as a phoenix rising from the ashes; — Becoming a leading eco-city (i.e. being a showcase); — Creating a liveable community for higher-income groups; — Proving that sustainability does not come with sacrificing luxury or comfort.
ACTORS	— Special purpose entity for European Housing Expo (Bo01 AB) with strong mandate; — Foundation and workings of Owners' Group in which Bo01 AB, the City of Malmö, and developers negotiated about the plan for Bo01; — Many architects and developers involved: diversity in construction and housing types; — Little citizen participation.
RESOURCES	— City of Malmö recovered costs through development agreements (land sales); — Local Investment Programme and European Union funding built financial leverage for the realization of bold objectives.
RULES	— General commitment to Quality Programme; — Generic rules on energy demand; — Generic rules on biodiversity (green points. green space factor).

Fig. 3.10 ↑ Neighbourhood arrangement of Bo01.

Fig. 3.11 Public amenity in the front, density in the back.

Regent Park
Toronto, Canada

Fig. 3.12 Facts and figures on the Regent Park Revitalization

Area 28 hectares

Start date 2006

Expected year of completion 2029

Expected population approx. 17,000 (original population: 7,500)

Project budget approx. 1 billion Canadian dollars
(original budget: approx. 500 million Canadian dollars)

Actors involved
— Toronto Community Housing (lead developer)
— The Daniels Corporation (developer)
— City of Toronto (partner for provision of childcare facilities,
  parks and recreation, and Regent Park Community Centre)
— Province of Ontario (funding provider for Pam McConnell
  Aquatic Centre, Daniels Spectrum, affordable housing)
— Federal Government of Canada (funding
  provider for Pam McConnell Aquatic Centre,
  Daniels Spectrum, affordable housing)
— Artscape (partner for Daniels Spectrum)
— CRC Regent Park Community Food Centre (partner for
  40 Oaks—affordable housing and community hub)
— Chartwell (developer for The Sumach—seniors housing)
— Dixon Hall (partner for Dixon Hall Youth Centre)
— MLSE Foundation (partner for Regent Park Athletic Grounds)

Fig. 3.13 Timeline: key decisions and actions in the Regent Park Revitalization

1995 ● Tenants approach housing corporations about revitalization of Regent Park (first, but failed attempt)

2002 ● Foundation of TCHC, later renamed to TCH

TCH takes initiative for community engagement towards plan for revitalization; intense participation process unfolds

2003 ● Toronto City Council approves revitalization

2006 ● TCH selects Daniels as development partner for Phase 1 after public Request For Proposal (RFP) process that was launched in December 2005

Phase 1 construction begins

2007 ● Toronto City Council passes Social Development Plan, developed in collaboration with original residents of Regent Park

2009 ● TCH grants Daniels a contract for all remaining phases

Phase 2 construction begins

2012 ● Phase 1 completed

2013 ● TCH scraps contract with Daniels for all remaining phases

2014 ● City Council approves alterations in revitalization plan, including shifting of densities and re-phasing from six to five phases in total

Phase 3 construction begins

2017 ● Phase 2 completed

2018 ● RFP launched for Phases 4 and 5

2023 ○ Phase 3 completed (estimated)

The Rebirth of Regent Park as a Mixed Neighbourhood

PREVIOUS USE
–

CONSTRUCTION TIME
2006–2029 (expected)

POPULATION
17,000 (expected)

HOMES
7,500 (expected)

AREA
28 hectares

→ Regent Park's original layout had only a few streets and was barely connected to the rest of the city. A more permeable street pattern (—) and a high quality of (public) amenity (▇) were two major components of the plan for the revitalization.

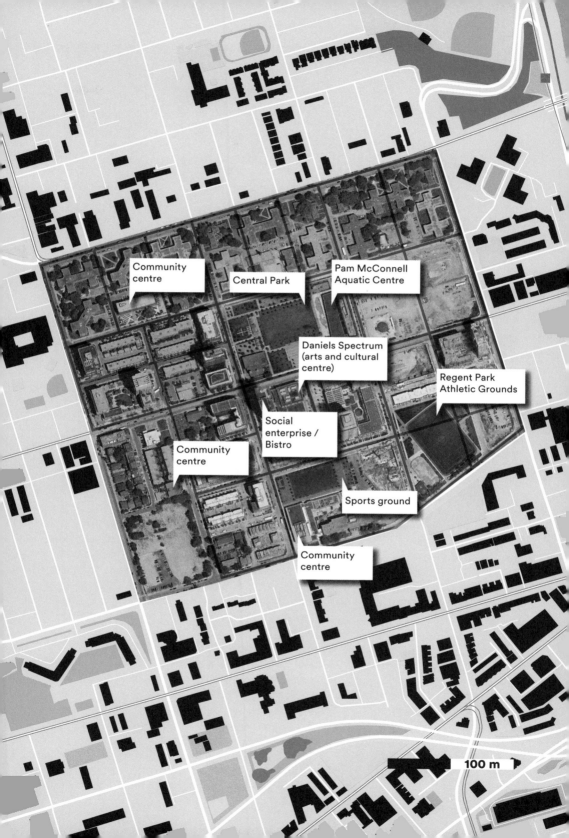

Fig. 3.14 ↑ Aerial view of
Regent Park in 1968: mid-rise
superblocks in a Garden City
setting (top half of the image)
combined with townhouses and
Le Corbusier-style high-rise
urbanism (bottom half).

Fig. 3.15 → Regent Park South
in 1968: towers in the park.

Its designers had the idea that it would become a safe and family-friendly neighbourhood for both low-income workers and soldiers returning from the battlefields across the Atlantic. In the decades after its construction, a different future unfolded. By the end of the twentieth century, Toronto's Regent Park had become deteriorated and riddled with crime. Indeed, like for many other neighbourhoods in the global North, the promises of modern city planning had ended in disappointment.

Through the peculiar combination of the long-term commitment of a private developer and a right to return for its original residents, Regent Park reinvented itself. Much of the neighbourhood was demolished between 2006 and today, and a rebuilt version of it appeared. Regent Park is now more densely populated and has a diverse set of amenities on offer. And many original Regent Parkers still live there. What happened? This chapter illuminates the planning process that made the overhaul of Regent Park possible. Who were the critical actors and what kind of nifty planning instruments were used to enable the reconstruction? We explain the successes of this planning approach and address the pitfalls and risks that have come up or are likely to do so in the longer term.

From 'a Superhighway of Crack Dealing'...

Regent Park was conceived as a 'community of the future' when it was built in the 1940s and 1950s. It was Canada's first large-scale public housing project and cleared Cabbagetown, 'the largest Anglo-Saxon slum in North America', as Toronto-based novelist Hugh Garner put it.[1] In Regent Park, working-class families were to find clean, private, and spacious homes.[2] As a set of mid-rise superblocks without through-streets, the neighbourhood was taken off Toronto's street grid. This urban morphology would provide plenty of open space to create a family-friendly environment for those living in the 2,000 social housing units in the neighbourhood.[3]

By 1997, its condition and reputation had become dire. Regent Park had very few commercial offerings and was a hotbed for drug-related crime and gang violence. A police officer characterized one of the neighbourhood's arterial roads as a 'superhighway of crack dealing'.[4] Once a celebrated public housing development, it had become a place of embarrassment for the city. 70 percent of the residents lived on a low income, and the neighbourhood had a long history of high unemployment.[5]

[1] H. Garner, *Cabbagetown* (Richmond Hill, ON: Simon & Schuster, 2017), p. 7.

[2] R.K. James, 'From "Slum Clearance" to "Revitalisation": Planning, Expertise and Moral Regulation in Toronto's Regent Park', *Planning Perspectives* 25, no. 1 (2010), pp. 69–86.

[3] L.C. Johnson and R.E. Johnson, *Regent Park Redux: Reinventing Public Housing in Canada* (London/New York: Routledge, 2017).

[4] CBC News, *Regent Park focus* [news item], 1997. Available at: http://bit.do/fJKgD (accessed 20 November 2018).

[5] Statistics Canada, & Land Information Toronto, *Regent Park (72). Social profile #3: Neighbourhoods. Households & Income* (Toronto: City of Toronto, 2004). And: S. Purdy, '"Ripped Off" by the System: Housing Policy, Poverty, and Territorial Stigmatization in Regent Park Housing Project, 1951–1991', *Labour/Le Travail* 52 (2003), pp. 45–108.

Fig. 3.16 ↑ Children play between the 'towers in the park' in 2012 (the towers were demolished later).

Why did Regent Park not live up to its promises? As has often been the case with modernist planning, principles of urban design did not connect to the lived experience of residents. When the first residents started moving on to other parts of the city in the 1960s, the neighbourhood of the future started to show its weaknesses. The inward-facing units, away from the streets, facilitated a 'no man's land' conducive to criminal activity in the open spaces between the buildings. The lack of through-streets and the abundance of culs-de-sac and pedestrian zones helped drug dealers to evade the police. In the meantime, residents suffered under the principle of single-use zoning: the neighbourhood ecology was monotonous and poor, requiring residents to get their groceries, social amenities, and recreational facilities elsewhere in Toronto. Provincial and city governments would systematically and categorically bicker over funding to support public housing projects, resulting in structural deficits in maintenance and operational budgets, as well as repair backlogs across the board—decrepit buildings, leaky apartments, mould build-up.

...to 'a Regular Neighbourhood'
Fast forward to 2019. Regent Park is no longer a 'backward' neighbourhood that Torontonians tend to avoid. The new Regent Park surprises many visitors. If it wasn't for a few remaining apartment blocks between Gerrard Street East and Oak Street—scheduled for demolition—that act as relics of a distant past, outsiders would think the old Regent Park never existed. At first sight, the change is most visible in the altered urban design. In a somewhat ironic turn of events, *tabula rasa* planning has eradicated the modern cityscape and brought streets back in. The streetscape now includes twenty-four blocks and through-streets, as opposed to two superblocks in the old design. The pre-war street pattern and connectivity to adjacent neighbourhoods and the rest of the city have been restored.[6] The superblocks have been demolished, and the uniformity of their brick buildings has been replaced by a mix of townhouses, mid-rises, and condominium towers. Importantly, densities have increased significantly: 2,083 existing social housing units are being replaced by as many new units for the original dwellers. On top of that, almost 5,500 market rental and ownership units will be added to the housing stock. Between 2006 and 2029, the number of dwellings is expected to grow from 2,083 to approximately 7,500, and the population increases from around 7,500 to at least 15,000 and probably as high as 17,000.[7]

We reflect on the metamorphosis of Regent Park with Ken Greenberg in his apartment on

[6] Toronto Community Housing, *Regent Park Urban Design Guidelines* (Toronto: Toronto Community Housing, 2005).

[7] Toronto Community Housing, *Regent Park*, 2018. Available at: http://bit.do/fJKgF (accessed 17 October 2018).

Fig. 3.17 ↑ A basketball field over-looked by Regent Park high-rises.

Fig. 3.18 (Next spread) Gardening space on the roof of a TCH building in 2018.

the southwestern end of downtown Toronto. Greenberg, an internationally well-known urban designer, said: 'We ended up with probably the best neighbourhood in terms of facilities.' Indeed, one indicator of the success is that people now come from outside the neighbour-hood to use the facilities, including an aquatic centre, an arts and cultural space, a central park, a new community centre, an affordable housing and community hub, and a cricket pitch and athletic grounds, all of which have been developed between 2012 and 2016. Various businesses have come to the neighbourhood: a FreshCo supermarket, a Tim Hortons coffee shop, and—the pride of its planners—a branch of the Royal Bank of Canada, the first bank to come to Regent Park in six-ty years. Other new facilities and retailers include pharmacies, restaur-ants, George Brown College, day-care centres, and a birth centre. And the list continues to get longer. The land use in the area has become mixed and the development of new community facilities has rendered the neighbourhood accessible and attractive to a wider public.

Another crucial difference with the past is in the social makeup of the neighbourhood. Regent Park no longer solely consists of public housing. A large majority of units are sold and rented out at market rates. About 25 percent of the future stock has been reserved

Fig. 3.19 ↑ Gardening space on the roof of a TCH building in 2018.

for public housing.[8] While all old super-blocks are being torn down, the original residents have been granted the right to return to their neighbourhood and live in brand new public housing buildings against similar rental fees. And so, while their new community is remarkably different from the one they left, both physically and socially, they are not by default being displaced. This is what makes the 'Regent Park Revitalization', its official title, unlike many urban renewal operations. While the rate of public housing units versus market housing units drops, in absolute terms the new Regent Park will have almost as many public housing homes as the pre-2006 Regent Park. It has become a mixed-income and mixed-tenure neighbourhood with an even stronger diversity record than it had.

The quality of the social housing apartment buildings is high. Regent Park's tenure-blind streetscape makes it difficult for visitors to distinguish between subsidized housing, market-priced townhouses and apartment buildings, shows Sureya Ibrahim when she takes us for a stroll around the neighbourhood. Ibrahim moved to Regent Park in the late 1990s and has made it her home. Working at the Centre of Learning & Development in the heart of the neighbourhood, she is a local community organizer. Apart from the car park underneath the condo towers, she says, she is not able to tell the different housing tenures in the buildings.

[8] In the Canadian context, social housing includes both subsidized housing and affordable rental. Subsidized housing is also called rent-geared-to-income (RGI) housing, where households pay up to thirty percent of their monthly income to rent—the rest of the rent is paid by TCH, as a government subsidy. Affordable rental implies that rents do not exceed eighty percent of the average market rent as set by the City of Toronto and the Canada Mortgage and Housing Corporation. Most TCH units (ninety percent, or approximately 54,000) are subsidized; affordable rental accounts for about 1,000 TCH units, and market-rate rental for 5,000. D. Vincent, '2,773 Applicants, Seventy-five Units: Inside Toronto's Affordable Housing Lottery', *Toronto Star*, 25 October 2018. Available at: http://bit.do/fJKgN (accessed 9 September 2019).

[9] City of Toronto, *Toronto Official Plan* (Toronto: City of Toronto, 2015).

Jed Kilbourn, senior development manager at TCH (Toronto Community Housing) and a member of the project team for the revitalization, shows us the top floor of a new TCH apartment building, at 230 Sackville Street. It has a common space that offers plenty of room for meetings and celebrations, as well as a fully equipped kitchen and a rooftop garden with plots to grow vegetables → Fig. 3.18 & Fig. 3.19. Like all common areas of the new TCH apartment buildings, we observe high-grade finishes. 'We wanted to create great environments for people to live in', Kilbourn says. That is what makes the project emblematic to him, especially considering the local government's conservative attitude to spending tax money on physical operations like this one.

The transformation of Regent Park into a thriving neighbourhood is surprising and unique. How did planners such as Jed Kilbourn and Ken Greenberg realize the transformation of Regent Park? What was the role of the community in this process? And how were the vast resources made available to finance it all?

Fig. 3.20 ↑ Residents hanging out in front of activist signs.

Fig. 3.21 ↘ Diverse groups of residents show up for local markets.

In this chapter, we will answer these questions by analyzing the history of Regent Park and exposing (the making of) its neighbourhood arrangement.

The Wealth of Community

Toronto self-identifies with diversity. 'As in nature, diversity is key to our social, cultural, and economic life. Diversity is our strength because it means vibrancy, opportunity, inclusiveness and adaptability', reads the operational 2015 Toronto Official Plan. It considers diversity a fundamental building block for the city's success just as much as the Plan of the mid-1990s did.[9] At the turn of the millennium, almost sixty languages were spoken in Regent Park. It was a poor neighbourhood, but it housed a solitary community with a strong identity. Long-term tenants characterized their place as lively and robust. Residents had always been involved in shaping the character of their neighbourhood, despite Regent Park being a classic result of mid-twentieth century top-down planning and development. Back in the day, it had been residents who raised money and rallied city hall to build the first community centre in the neighbourhood. The popular skating rink had been the pet project of a Regent Park local; he started flooding a parking lot in one of the ice-cold Toronto winters and never stopped doing it. Dozens of social-service organizations had established in the area over time, including the Christian Resource Centre, the Community Health Centre, and artistic and educational communities. Regent Park clearly was home to social capital and entrepreneurship. And there was awareness among residents that something had to change in their neighbourhood. They lobbied actively for physical reconstruction as the built form of their area fostered crime and created unsafe spaces.[10]

Early attempts to redevelop Regent Park originated within the community, including a 1996 proposal aimed at demolishing and replacing hundreds of units.[11] While plans like these were usually shelved, this 1996 attempt gained momentum and achieved the phase in which levels of government were in the same room with residents. It seemed to set the stage for something big, but the provincial government of Ontario—which owned the Regent Park projects at that time—refused to commit capital funds, thus effectively blocking urban renewal.

Established in 2002 and committed to being a new kind of public housing landlord, Toronto Community Housing launched a process to formulate a masterplan for the revitalization of Regent Park.[12] A team of consultants, including John Gladki and Ken Greenberg, were assigned to establish a vision and principles ultimately leading to official plans. Moreover, the public housing corporation felt a need to design and implement a community process that would be welcomed by residents and win their confidence, empowering the population to meaningfully engage in building their own future community. And so TCH contracted consultants for a community engagement process. Ken Greenberg looks back: 'We went without drawing a single line and we started a series of conversations with the people in Regent Park.' The four key questions residents were asked were: what do you like about Regent Park, what don't you like, what do you hope for, and what do you fear? Sometimes conversations would not bear any relevance to the planning process, but improving the neighbourhood was always in the back of people's minds, because the goal was to consider what a revitalized Regent Park might look like. Extensive series of meetings and interactions in various forms and settings took place with the help of

[10] S. Meagher and T. Boston, *Community Engagement and the Regent Park Redevelopment* (Toronto: Toronto Community Housing, 2003).

[11] Johnson and Johnson, *Regent Park Redux*, 2017, p. 46.

[12] In the late 1990s, the government of the Province of Ontario, then led by Mike Harris, downloaded its public housing responsibilities to municipalities. Furthermore, in 1998 two housing corporations that were active in Toronto, being the Metropolitan Toronto Housing Company and the City of Toronto Non-Profit Housing Corporation, merged into the Toronto Housing Company and were put under the auspices of the City of Toronto. A merger between this company and the Metropolitan Toronto Housing Corporation eventually established the Toronto Community Housing Corporation (TCHC) in 2002, which was later renamed to TCH.

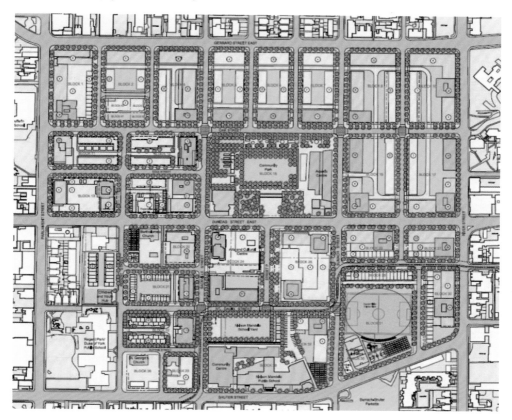

Fig. 3.22 ↑ A new layout for Regent Park, to be developed in five phases: more through streets and a mix of townhouses, mid-rise buildings and tall buildings.

appointed 'community animators': community-based workers who represented the population's main ethnic and cultural groups. Sean Meagher, who co-designed the community engagement process, explains how he and his colleagues broke the process down structurally, anticipating that Somalis tended to gather in big meetings while Spanish residents liked to gather around kitchen tables.[13] TCH invested significantly in seeking advice and cooperation from residents, and the conclusions of the consultation process were straightforward: 'We want to be a neighbourhood just like any other neighbourhood. We don't want to be isolated and poor, or separated', is what the residents said.

The results of the community engagement process were captured in a list of twelve leading community planning principles for the revitalization.[14] Key principles were to create a neighbourhood with a mix of uses, including a range of housing → Fig. 3.22, employment, institutions, and services, and to keep the same number of subsidized housing units. Residents were of the opinion that they had a right of return, and they had a powerful advocate for their electoral district, the late

[13] S. Micallef, *Regent Park: A Story of Collective Impact* (Toronto: Metcalf Foundation, 2013).

[14] Toronto Community Housing, *Regent Park Community Update Meeting, 19 April, 2018.* Available at: http://bit.do/fJKhN (accessed 2 December 2018).

Pam McConnell, who stood behind them and successfully insisted on a binding, legal right of return. The right was legally and politically entrenched before the first shovel hit the ground in Regent Park.[15] It was included in the Toronto Official Plan,[16] and the Regent Park Secondary Plan.[17] And so TCH had to commit to the principle of the right of return: any resident who would be temporarily displaced would have the right to move back to Regent Park once new housing would become available—with rent calculated the same way as before. In 2005, the City of Toronto and TCH signed a Section 37 agreement, a contract that focused strongly on protecting the rights of the original residents as it outlined meticulously the legal obligations tied to the right of return. Also, the City of Toronto approved zoning by-laws that allowed to implement the right of return and ensured regulating and monitoring of the redevelopment process. In one of the latest accounts on the relocating and returning of residents, Shauna Brail and Nishi Kumar report that by early 2016 almost 1,300 households had moved out of their old homes to make way for the redevelopment. About half of this group had returned to new housing in Regent Park, a tenth had left TCH, and another tenth had waived their right of return. The remaining households were then still based in temporary housing, waiting for their turn to go back or decide otherwise.[18]

The Toronto City Council approved the principle of revitalizing Regent Park in the summer of 2003[19] and gave the decisive green light in 2005.[20] One appeal was filed with the Ontario Municipal Board, the then adjudicative tribunal for applications and appeals on municipal and planning disputes. The dispute was settled and after a short hearing the plan was approved. After this decision, the engagement of residents remained important. The 2007 Social Development Plan (SDP) identified the needs of the community and made a case for better education, more jobs, and more amenities.

Crumbling Buildings, Cash-Strapped Corporations, and the Turn to Private Capital

Rebuilding a neighbourhood from the ground up is costly. TCH was not in a position to initiate it on its own. While the housing corporation had a plan, it also had empty pockets. In the early 2000s, TCH faced a major repair backlog that was bound to increase further—it had inherited this backlog from its predecessors. Moreover, it was short of hundreds of millions of Canadian dollars

(15) M. August, 'It's all about power and you have none: The marginalization of tenant resistance to mixed-income social housing redevelopment in Toronto, Canada', *Cities* 56 (2016), pp. 25–32.

(16) City of Toronto, *Toronto Official Plan* (Toronto: City of Toronto, 2010).

(17) City of Toronto, *Regent Park Secondary Plan* (Toronto: City of Toronto, 2007).

(18) S. Brail and N. Kumar, 'Community leadership and engagement after the mix: the transformation of Toronto's Regent Park', *Urban Studies* 54, no. 16 (2017), pp. 3772–3788.

(19) City of Toronto, *Regent Park Revitalization: City Actions (Toronto Centre-Rosedale, Ward 28). Meeting of the Council of the City of Toronto on 22, 23, and 24 July, 2003* (Toronto: City of Toronto, 2003).

(20) City of Toronto, *Final Report: Application to Amend the Official Plan and Zoning By-law – Regent Park Revitalization: Toronto Community Housing Corporation (Toronto Centre-Rosedale, Ward 28). Meeting of the Council of the City of Toronto on 1, 2, and 3 February, 2005* (Toronto: City of Toronto, 2005).

(21) TCH has continued to struggle financially more recently as well. In 2014 it was calculated that TCH needed 2.6 billion Canadian dollars to upkeep its 58,500 housing units—an amount it did not have at its disposal at the time. TV Ontario (2014) *The Agenda with Steve Paikin.* Available at: http://bit.do/fJKhT (accessed 20 November 2018). Furthermore, in a 2016 report from the Mayor's Task Force on Toronto Community Housing, the housing corporation was claimed to be 'an unsustainable corporation' that was 'not financially sustainable in its present form'. City of Toronto, *Transformative change for TCHC: A Report from the Mayor's Task Force on Toronto Community Housing* (Toronto: City of Toronto, 2016), p. 18.

to upkeep its portfolio.[21] The corporation's struggles rooted in decades of federal, provincial, and local housing policies that had been aimed at efficiency gains in the housing sector—chronic budget cuts and the shifting of responsibilities from provinces to municipalities. It became increasingly clear that a reconsideration of public housing policy in Toronto was needed, and this exercise was to include recalculations of the financial model behind this policy.

With its foundation in 2002, TCH inherited a long waiting list of qualified potential residents, gained control over an obsolete portfolio, and stumbled on a structural shortage of funds. Against this backdrop, from the start, the corporation began to explore avenues of alternative and innovative financing. John Gladki explains:

> TCH is wholly owned by the City [of Toronto], but it has a board which is at arm's length from the city administration. So it has some flexibility to do things that agencies that are departments of the city could not do normally.

In this sweet spot, TCH's first director, Derek Ballantyne, initiated a process of rethinking, bearing in mind that if governments would not help TCH out, then the private sector had to step forward. Also, Ballantyne convinced the City of Toronto to float a bond for the housing corporation, which provided more financial leeway and opened extra doors for the renewal of Regent Park.

'Just assume the whole thing is a blank slate.' If Gladki recalls correctly, that is what TCH director Ballantyne said at the time. As a CEO he had already decided early on that *that* had to happen: to start considering Regent Park as an asset which had value—a land asset. The idea was to bring private capital into TCH's system and put public housing on a new footing. With Toronto's thriving downtown only a half-hour walk to the West, Regent Park had an impeccable potential for private-sector-led development and investment. To raise the funds needed for neighbourhood revitalization, TCH was considering selling or trading land and development rights. Furthermore, a radical rebuild would put the newly founded housing corporation in the picture and mark its great ambitions. In Gladki's words, Ballantyne also saw that 'he needed a masterplan as a way of galvanizing interest, needed excitement in moving it ahead, and … needed the support of the community'.

[22] Cresford Developments won the bid that had been announced in 2005, but gave back the assignment before coming to a contractual agreement with TCH. Planner John Gladki about Cresford: 'They were determined to move with it and wanted to make it happen, but they just were not big enough and were not willing to take the risk.'

Densifying and Mixing for Affordability

Not having the capital to redevelop Regent Park gradually—let alone the staff or expertise—to dare consider this a solo performance, TCH started exploring ways of using its land ownership in the neighbourhood as leverage for building a consortium or consortia with the private sector. A partner had to be found, and a business case had to be built. A cumbersome procurement process ensued, including a failed tender in the spring of 2005 and significant changes in terms of the assignment that was on the table.[22] Eventually, TCH found a consortium partner in The Daniels Corporation (hereafter: Daniels). TCH initially selected Daniels as a development partner for Phase 1. In 2009 the assignment was extended to all remaining phases. However, in 2013 TCH made the decision to scrap this extended assignment and re-open the bidding process for Phases 4 and 5. This decision was not made public before 2018.

To render a TCH's desired *tabula rasa* financially feasible, the consortium partners—TCH and Daniels—figured that a new social mix for the neighbourhood was the way go to. Densifying Regent Park into a mixed-income, mixed-tenure neighbourhood would help TCH in upgrading the area and allow for Daniels to recoup their investment. Portions of the proceeds from the sales of market housing, together with operating and capital maintenance savings and local government contributions towards infrastructure, would fund the construction of new social housing units. And so the provision of social housing, TCH's core business, came to be premised on developing and selling market housing. Daniels expected that they had to build and sell 3,000 market housing units to cover the costs of building 2,083 public housing units and retain a reasonable rate of return. 'The math looked promising', Toronto-based journalist John Lorinc wrote in a 2013 piece in the *University of Toronto Magazine*.[23] But it also required a bold demolition-and-build operation. Fast sales and high revenues could speed up the delivery of public housing and generate a higher budget for TCH in the revitalization project—for instance, to forestall potential setbacks such as rising construction costs. 'We entered into a co-tenancy arrangement... where we co-created a development corporation', says Jed Kilbourn as he addresses some institutional specifics about Phase 1 and Phase 2 of the project. The co-tenancy built the buildings and sold them to the market; it was a profit-share model in which profits were divided between Daniels and TCH. In 2014, TCH decided to enter into a land sale model with Daniels: 'We sell land to them, use the profit of the land sale to fund our development and they act as our construction managers', Kilbourn explains.

The Math Revisited

The math did not work as hoped.[24] The Regent Park Revitalization has faced persistent funding challenges since its conception, a struggle that has been reported widely in the press.[25] Back in 2003, TCH and the City of Toronto foresaw a 55 million Canadian dollar deficit: the construction costs of the social housing units were projected to be 455 million Canadian dollars, against revenues of about 400 million. The difference would be

[23] J. Lorinc, 'The New Regent Park: A University Community Helps a Neighbourhood Transform', *University of Toronto Magazine*, 27 March 2013. Available at: http://bit.do/fJKhU (accessed 2 December 2018).

[24] J. Lorinc, 'Final Phases of Regent Park Redevelopment to Be Open to Tender', *The Globe and Mail*, 16 May 2018. Available at: http://bit.do/fJKhV (accessed 7 April 2019).

[25] S. Brail and A. Jean-Baptiste, 'What TCHC Needs to Do Next with Regent Park', *Spacing Toronto*, 25 June 2018. Available at: http://bit.do/fJKhY (accessed 1 November 2018); S. Levy, 'Regent Park Revitalization $107 Million in the Hole', *Toronto Sun*, 29 January 2017. Available at: http://bit.do/fJKh2 (accessed 3 December 2017); A. McKeen, 'Why Regent Park's Revitalization Needs $108 Million More to Keep Going', *Torontoist*, 6 February 2017. Available at: http://bit.do/fJKh3 (accessed 20 November 2018).

provided by the local public purse, through TCH. More recent estimations of the financial gap drew a dramatically different picture, though:
the overall project costs increased to 1 billion Canadian dollars, and
the funding shortfall grew to 200 million in 2018. TCH had not seen a
deficit of this size coming.[26]

The revitalization became expensive for several reasons.
First, it simply became more expensive to build public housing units.
Changes in the building code, like improved accessibility requirements, and rising construction costs, in general due to increased
demand as a result of the heated real estate market, contributed to the
increase in costs. The total revenues shrunk, and so did the amount of
money that went to TCH as part of the profit-share model. In one of
her 2017 *Torontoist* articles, Alex McKeen adds that delays in the sales
of market housing units put a hold on social housing redevelopment,
which increased the relocation costs borne by TCH.[27]

The math for the revitalization required an overhaul.
Further densification became the adage for TCH and Daniels. While
the original plan indicated 2,083 units of social housing against approximately 3,000 market units, the latter had increased to well over
5,400 in 2019—with the number of social housing units remaining
at a steady 2,083. The logic behind this shift was as simple as it was
radical: more market units were needed to cover the costs of building
social housing units. The funding model once took off with a 1:1.5 ratio
between social housing and market housing, but in 2013 it was calculated that Daniels needed to build 3 to 4 market units for every single
social housing unit to offset the costs.

Regent Park went from 75 dwellings per hectare in the
old days to 260 in the newest plans. Keir Brownstone of TCH admits
that although the initial concept of density for the revitalization was
fairly intense already at 180 dwellings per hectare, the developers
involved have been asking for more and more. The most controversial
increase in density was approved by the City of Toronto in 2013, after
TCH and Daniels had proposed to increase the total number of units
to approximately 7,500. It would bring the projected population from
12,500 to 17,000 and include the adding of several tall buildings.[28]
Critics contended that the revitalized Regent Park would suffer from
overcrowding and insufficient public transit, but the additional densification happened anyway.

Regent Park now is a neighbourhood where people
want to buy property. In the Regent Park Presentation Centre, on the
corner of Dundas Street and Regent Street, it is a coming-and-going of
potential buyers. People from widely different cultural
backgrounds orient themselves on the units that are for
sale. Inside you can feel their sense of excitement as
they organize photos to be taken of them—with the big
model of the new urban layout of Regent Park in front
of them, of course. In the coffee corner we see a couple
of people sipping americanos. They could never afford

[26] Lorinc, 'Final Phases of
Regent Park Redevelopment
to Be Open to Tender', 2018.

[27] McKeen, 'Why Regent Park's
Revitalization Needs $1 Million
More to Keep Going', 2017.

[28] Johnson and Johnson,
Regent Park Redux, 2017.

Fig. 3.23 ↑ Project: Pam McConnell Aquatic Centre (formerly named Regent Park Aquatic Centre).

to buy one of the apartments but can afford to live in Regent Park nevertheless.

But the planners' dream of a newly developed, mixed neighbourhood came at a cost. Admittedly, by selling pieces of land to Daniels, TCH limited its exposure to market risk. These land sales enabled the housing corporation to secure land value upfront and unlock funding earlier and—most importantly—to itself. It meant untying the social housing component of the project from the market housing component. Reducing risk also implied lower rewards, though, and sales are generally not a recipe for the best returns. The move to land-sale agreements for Phase 3 of the revitalization reduced projected returns for TCH and actually contributed to the funding gap. Jed Kilbourn explains that attitudes of TCH Boards of Directors toward risky behaviour have become more careful over the past two decades. Referring to the early 2000s, he says: 'I think the risk tolerance then was significantly different than the risk tolerance now', including a supportive Board of Directors and Derek Ballantyne as an engaging and supportive CEO.

Navigating to a Strong Neighbourhood Ecology
When it comes to the quality of the public domain, oftentimes high ambitions in the preparation stage of a plan erode as a project's implementation unfolds, just to retain the viability of a business case. But in Regent Park we see the opposite. 'The plan that was approved at that time does not exist today', Greg Spearn of TCH claimed in 2014 as he looked back on the 2002 masterplan. There was no athletic grounds, no swimming pool, no Daniels Spectrum. Spearn: 'All of that has happened as it has evolved over the years.'(29) Planner John Gladki plays down the importance of his own craft. 'You can plan all you want, but you have to leave room for magic to happen as the plan evolves, as the work evolves. And that is what has happened here.' High-quality streetscapes and finishes—sidewalks, paving, lighting, landscaping, trees—were on the agenda from the start and therefore incorporated into the original plan. And then layers of public domain were added.

The modern swimming pool that opened its doors in 2012 is a good example → Fig. 3.23. If it wasn't for Councillor Pam McConnell the pool would have never existed. She secured over two million Canadian dollars to build the facility by raising contributions using a Section 37 compromise in which a developer pays for the construction of something else in exchange for approval to build more floors. The development of a sixty-five-storey skyscraper in Toronto's Financial District was only approved after the developers had committed a contribution to McConnell's

(29) TV Ontario, *The Agenda*, 2014.

Fig. 3.24 ↑ Looking West, Regent Park Boulevard is one of the new streets that cross Dundas Street. And, unthinkable before 2006, there are places to grab a bite or have coffee in Regent Park.

Fig. 3.25 (Next spread) Overlooking Regent Park toward the neighbourhood park.

budget for her ward, which she forwarded to the City of Toronto so that the aquatic centre could be erected—an expenditure of 16.6 million Canadian dollars.[30]

The sense of flexibility among planners and urbanists has facilitated the Regent Park Revitalization to adapt, but Daniels have been the keenest driver of add-ons. The developer rallied for a centre for community representatives to meet, and reserved the corner of Dundas Street and Sackville Street for Paintbox Bistro, a social enterprise and catering and bistro hub. Having a background in developing non-profit co-operative housing, and being known for their ability to weave arts and culture into the community fabric, from the outset leaders and staff at Daniels aspired to go beyond a traditional bricks-and-mortar approach.[31] They became involved in many aspects of Regent Park's community life, building trust among the original residents through consulting them and showing a sincere interest in 'fixing' the neighbourhood—which meant more than just housing units and new residents.

The developer had an active recruitment and outreach strategy to take the neighbourhood's projected amenities to another level. They abandoned the rather conservative 2002 masterplan and embraced the 2007 Social Development Plan, which had been designed in its entirety by the Regent Park community.

[30] J. Warmington, 'McConnell a "Tough Negotiator": Trump', *Toronto Sun*, 8 July 2017. Available at: http://bit.do/fJKia (accessed 10 September 2019).

[31] Lorinc, 'The New Regent Park', 2013.

Fig. 3.26 ↑ Residents gather around a fire pit in Toronto's winter season.

Mitchell Cohen, President of The Daniels Corporation, had noticed a disconnect between the two plans.[32] He decided to embark on the SDP to harvest the cultural diversity of Regent Park. Cohen formed a non-profit joint-venture involving Daniels, TCH, and urban art organization Artscape to develop and operate Daniels Spectrum. Through fundraising campaigns, negotiation tactics, and their ability to tap into other creative forms of funding, Daniels enabled developments that were not obvious, given the context.[33] Then there is retail. 'Just the idea of having businesses come in was a struggle', says Keir Brownstone when we meet him in Paintbox Bistro. Ken Greenberg recalls that he and the other planners wanted a grocery store at the corner of Dundas Street and Parliament Street: 'All the market analysts had told us: "You will never get it, you will never get retail there." But we were stubborn and we put that in the Request for Proposal. And Daniels managed to come up with FreshCo.' They had had to twist arms for it, but in the end they succeeded.

Finally, Daniels rendered flexibility in the plan implementation by accelerating or re-phasing parts of the proposed development. The neighbourhood park → Fig. 3.25, centrally located in the community, was initially scheduled for construction in 2020. Mitchell Cohen did not like this outlook: the first new residents would have to wait almost a decade for proper public space.

[32] Johnson and Johnson, *Regent Park Redux*, 2017, p. 100.

[33] The construction of the Regent Park Athletic Grounds, for instance, was made possible by financial support (four million Canadian dollars) from the MLSE Foundation, which also provided operating money.

TCH and Daniels rejigged the phasing strategy and delivered the park mid-2014 instead, creating both value for future private developments and an amenity for the people who lived there from the start. The flexible plan as a magnet for other things.

And so community and planning strategies merged into a process that harnessed flexibility and somewhat ad-hoc amenity building, with recurring rezoning applications and changes to the original masterplan. Before each project phase, TCH and Daniels would look at details more closely and submit a development context plan. This method enabled the evolution of changes throughout the redevelopment *and* provided for an orderly sequencing of development and appropriate infrastructure and services. But how the plan evolved also happened at the expense of someone's purse. The richer neighbourhood ecology, with amenities such as parks, open spaces, a community centre, and an aquatic centre, did not burden TCH's budget, but certainly affected Daniels' business case, taking up land that had initially been zoned for housing. Density had to be moved around for the developer to keep achieving their targets. Initially, the vision had been to spread out the townhouses, mid-rise buildings, and towers across the project site. But since the density shifts took place tall building production has concentrated at the eastern edge of Regent Park.

A Transformation to a Green Future?

Regent Park illustrates how a neighbourhood arrangement can be effectively deployed to fundamentally change a neighbourhood ecology. There was the institutional birth of TCH and the decision to rebuild the neighbourhood from the ground up; an advanced community engagement process that indulged in the wealth of diversity and established a right of return; an effective but not undisputed business case that used land sales and commerce-driven density as levers toward welfare-oriented affordability and amenity. And the wisdom and ability of planners and others involved to change tack now and then, facilitated by a planning system that allowed things to evolve. These events and conditions have been pivotal and helped the operation of rebuilding Regent Park become a controversial attempt at building a better Toronto. It generated a high-quality neighbourhood in terms of the quality of housing, social mix, and the rich neighbourhood ecology with all sorts of amenities and services.

Climate and energy were no central concerns for planners and developers. They were a 'matter of course'. Unlike Bo01, a poster child for sustainability, Regent Park wanted to become 'a regular neighbourhood'. However, while everything seemed set for reaching climate and energy targets on the way, it so happens that Regent Park may have to undergo yet another dramatic transformation. From the looks of its metrics and building stock, Regent Park actually appears to be quite 'green' already: the buildings are built to LEED certification standards; there is plenty of parkland, which contributes to a natural infiltration of rainwater; an energy plant and district heating system that could run on regionally-sourced biomass are available; the urban design lends itself well to active transport, with short distances to public facilities and amenities; and homes come with 'smart' and energy-efficient devices—programmable thermostats, lighting, heating, and cooling systems. Yet the lived experience of the neighbourhood sketches a somewhat different picture. Smart buildings do not automatically make for an energy-neutral performance.

Keir Brownstone admits that he and his colleagues have underestimated the difficulties of making people adjust their behaviour to realize the energy performance that their buildings are technically capable of. Brownstone remembers walking outside a TCH building on a cold winter day at a temperature of fifteen degrees Celsius below zero. Yet he counted no less than ninety open windows. As an energy-saving tech enthusiast, he could not help thinking immediately of the costs and energy loss the residents were burdening their landlord (TCH) with. An important explanation for their 'grey' behaviour is that there is no individualized energy billing system in 95 percent of TCH's social housing units. TCH pays for the utility costs and tenants do not receive a report of their energy usage. But there is more. Intrigued by the fact that LEED-certified buildings did not at all perform as expected, Brownstone's boss went to a housing unit to look into a complaint from one of TCH's tenants. She was too cold in her unit, and it felt pretty chilly in her home indeed. Brownstone's boss pointed to the thermostat and said: 'Don't you use that?' The tenant responded: 'What would I use it for, it's a clock, isn't it?' It is a telling anecdote. The TCH residents of Regent Park are socially very mixed but smart technology often takes white middle-class inhabitants as users for granted. Of course, the apartment and thermostat had come with a manual. But it was a bulky book—and in English and French only. And, as many residents often change homes quickly, it had gone missing anyway. LEED-certified buildings and smart thermostats will not by default lead to green behaviour if its users are not taken into account. While the boldness of the demolition-and-build approach created an opportunity to 'fix' the neighbourhood, the physical operation has been ahead of the social transformation ever since the revitalization started.

Recapitulating the Arrangement: How Sustainable is It?

The revitalization has changed the ownership of Regent Park, both technically and figuratively. It started as a largely community-led, locally-based initiative, and brought in many newcomers and happenings over the past twenty years. It improved the level of amenity and increased the diversity in functions and housing tenures, but the condos and the boost in cultural and leisure offerings are very much the result of outside investments and interests that were a mere necessity to rebuild deteriorated public housing units. Ismail Afrah, a young Regent Park resident, admits feeling confused about the revitalization:

[It is] about having to be in a community you identify with, but at the same time, because you see the total change that is happening.... It feels at the same time that this is not an output you're giving.... So even though you might feel a sense of gratefulness, a sense of joy, that things are changing ... at the same time you're concerned that these are not for you.[34]

Jael Cabey Jones, a Regent Park local who stars in the 2017 documentary *My Piece of the City* about the neighbourhood's young artists,[35] puts it more bluntly in *The Globe and Mail*: 'I feel like they stomped all over Regent Park and said, basically: "Your history is not good enough for us to want to keep."'[36]

While the revitalization of Regent Park has become an exemplar of urban regeneration, the underlying business model is struggling, as is TCH's financial *modus operandi*. And so, there is uncertainty about the project's long-term contribution. Indisputably, without the formula of densification for affordability and amenity, the new Regent Park had never existed. But there is a cost, as to what degree extensive densification serves the purpose of making better places. A total of 17,000 people (current estimations) will be residing in the twenty-eight-hectare neighbourhood. At this level of density, living in Regent Park will be more intense. Regardless of this density complex, the viability of the operation, even of the neighbourhood as such, requires critical consideration: this revitalization has mainly been a one-time injection of capital. It is the sale of the homes and the land that finance the construction of public housing, but there is not more money going into operating and maintaining buildings owned by TCH. And at some point, TCH will not be able to sell off more land. While brand new housing has been and will be delivered, the funding challenges for TCH remain just as daunting. The financial sustainability on the part of TCH is a real concern: operation and maintenance costs will never disappear and are likely to increase, but there is a finite amount of money coming in from the proceeds of the Regent Park sales.

It is tricky math. But Jed Kilbourn sees a situation where TCH and the City of Toronto would never have done anything and just continued to maintain the buildings. As he contemplates the question, he admits he observes a fundamental problem with selling public land to repair existing housing stock. However, he also states:

[W]e managed to not invest in this [neighbourhood] for sixty years and let people sit in sub-standard housing. So, what's the better alternative right now? I am not interested in debates about the effect of

[34] S. Fernandes, *Informal Social Relationships in a Newly Mixed Income Community: A Regent Park Case Study* [Master's thesis] (Waterloo, ON: University of Waterloo, 2014), p. 105. Available at: http://bit.do/fJKif (accessed 20 November 2018).

[35] M. Mossanen (director), M. Cohen, and H. Omarkhail (producers), *My Piece of the City* (documentary), 2017.

[36] M. Vincent, 'Documentary Looks at Regent Park Community's Response to Revitalization', *The Globe and Mail*, 16 November 2017. Available at: http://bit.do/fJKii (accessed 1 November 2018).

neoliberalism on a public asset. And this is where the planner in me comes to the fore. I need to do something to improve the situation. And if this is the mechanism for doing it, then I would at least want for the public agency to have a very strong hand in the development.

This is where the main critique of the revitalization surfaces. If Toronto continues to disinvest in social housing like it has done in the past sixty years, by 2080 Regent Park is in a situation as dire and its buildings as crumbling as they were in the early 2000s. With the difference that TCH will have sold many of its assets and thus have nothing to trade. There have been ebbs and flows of funding for public housing in the past sixty years, and the abilities of TCH and its predecessors to respond to housing challenges have been largely dependent on the generosity of political movers and shakers. As for Regent Park, TCH's ability has even become dependent on market tendencies and business outlooks on the part of The Daniels Corporation.

Unless dramatic decisions are made to reform TCH's funding model and operating structure, the economic sustainability of public housing rebuilds in Toronto remains thin. The business model designed for the Regent Park Revitalization thrives on hard markets, not soft ones and so Toronto's strong real estate market was of great help to selling market housing quickly, paving the way for new public housing to be financed, built, and used. That is the main caveat of the model, says also Jennifer Keesmaat, former chief planner at the City of Toronto: 'This is a model that only works when there is a really hot market and you have properties that are in desirable areas.'[37] Regent Park has been piggybacking the city that welcomes tens of thousands of new residents every year, using its proximity to the bustling downtown as a selling point. This context implies an inherent challenge to transferring the lessons learned in Regent Park to other locales. The opportunity to do market-based development is not as great in weaker, softer markets, but all the more interesting in well-located neighbourhoods in over-pressured cities.

[37] D. Hayes, 'Inside Regent Park: Toronto's Test Case for Public-Private Gentrification', *The Guardian*, 8 December 2016. Available at: http://bit.do/fJKiq (accessed 17 October 2018).

DISCOURSE	— 'We want to be a neighbourhood just like any other neighbourhood.'
ACTORS	— Newly-formed housing corporation starts considering land as an asset with market potential; — Community engagement process provides residents a sense of ownership; — Developer's approach goes beyond bricks-and-mortar; — Planners and consultants involved remain open to change and new ideas.
RESOURCES	— Land sales and densification provide leverage for affordability and amenity; — Housing corporation can sell land only once; revitalization is essentially a one-time injection of cash and does not involve (long-term) maintenance and operations; — Cost overruns and time delays burden project budget and increase need for higher densities, with housing corporation depending on political decisionmakers.
RULES	— Right of return for residents of all 2,083 original housing units; — Planning rules allow for stop-and-go moments between development phases to calibrate and amend plans.

Fig. 3.27 ↑ Neighbourhood arrangement for Regent Park.

Fig. 3.28 High-rise and public space are two defining aspects of Overvecht's morphology.

Overvecht
Utrecht,
the Netherlands

Fig. 3.29 Facts and figures on Overvecht

Area 440 hectares

....

Built 1960s

....

Number of residents approx. 35,000 (17,500 of whom reside in Overvecht-Noord)

....

Selection of actors involved
— City of Utrecht (in various roles, e.g. planner, landowner)
— National Government of the Netherlands (funding provider for plan to take homes off natural-gas grid)
— Bo-Ex, Mitros, Portaal (housing associations)
— Stedin (energy network operator)
— Energie-U (energy cooperative)
— Project team 'Overvecht-Noord Aardgasvrij' (on behalf of municipality, housing associations, Stedin, and Energie-U)
— Heijmans (developer) and other developers and investors
— Nieuwe Energie voor de Vechtzoom (bottom-up initiative on energy transition—led by residents)
— Platform for Residents

Fig. 3.30 Timeline: key developments in the history of Overvecht

1960s	Construction of Overvecht
Early 1990s	First signals of neighbourhood's downward spiral
2001	Presentation of De Utrechtse Opgave (The Utrecht Challenge), a plan for radical physical renewal in Overvecht—not implemented as planned
2000s – 2010s	Series of policy programmes—large and small—incorporating labour, health, education, safety, and poverty reduction into comprehensive social plans for Overvecht
2010s	Foundation of several initiatives and organizations that seek co-benefits, such as Bouw=Wouw (Construction=Cool), Plan Einstein, Project O, and Buurtbuik
2017	City of Utrecht announces Overvecht-Noord as testbed for energy transition, triggering sentiments of anger and anxiety from residents
2018	Community initiative in Overvecht-Noord to design a way forward in the energy transition
Fall 2018 – Spring 2019	Dedicated project team starts consultation process toward transition plan for Overvecht-Noord, including 'neighbourhood conversations'
Fall 2019	Transition plan for Overvecht-Noord
2030	Overvecht-Noord off natural gas (expected)

Learning from Overvecht – A Case for Social-ecological Renovation

Overvecht is a modernist neighbourhood, built in the Dutch city of Utrecht in the 1960s. Back then it was envisioned as a 'neighbourhood of tomorrow', delivering on the dreams of a healthy home for the post-war generations, a neighbourhood where people could live with dignity. Similar to modernist-built neighbourhoods elsewhere, what started with the best of intentions, lost its appeal over time. Bit by bit social problems grew. Many of those who could move, moved elsewhere, either within the city or to suburbia. Those who had no alternative remained. Currently, Overvecht is a typical example of what Dutch media euphemistically refer to as a 'vulnerable neighbourhood'. Many residents struggle to make ends meet, find a job, stay healthy, or feel at home in their neighbourhood.[1] Some landed in Overvecht because there was nowhere else to go. Remarkably

PREVIOUS USE
–

CONSTRUCTION TIME
1960s

POPULATION
35,000

HOMES
16,750

AREA
440 hectares

enough it was precisely the northern part of *this* neighbourhood that was selected to be a 'testbed' for the energy transition. By 2030 Overvecht-Noord should be completely off natural gas, which is now used for heating and cooking. So, here is modernist Overvecht, in the vanguard once again, but this time as a neighbourhood to showcase an energy transition.

The case of Overvecht is both intriguing and instructive. The challenge of converting post-war, underprivileged areas into climate-neutral neighbourhoods is as massive as it is urgent. Modernist high-rise neighbourhoods like Overvecht are common in Western Europe, each with its own spatial, social, and economic intricacies. What can we learn from Overvecht's first steps towards an energy transition?[2] Rather than as a best practice, we approach Overvecht as informative; a case in which we can see the many seemingly separate logics that are at play. Logics that must be appreciated and, wherever possible, connected to help create a successful neighbourhood.

The Case of Overvecht

Overvecht is home to about 35,000 inhabitants[3] and has the typical layout of the Dutch variation of modernist urbanism. Born out of idealism and an urge to break with traditionalism, the neighbourhood was set up along a geometrical grid, with high-rise apartment blocks (ten storeys), mid-rises (four storeys) and single-family dwellings (two storeys), which are scattered over hundreds of hectares in a low-density setting. In the original idea, the neighbourhood was to be home to a broad range of citizens, from blue-collar to white-collar workers.

Overvecht catered to a true need. There had been severe housing shortages in the post-war decades, and therefore young families were overwhelmed with joy when receiving the key to what was to be their first home or a considerable step up from the overly moist dwellings in the areas directly outside the inner city.[4] In the 1960s, Overvecht was the scene of post-war happiness with a neighbourhood ecology that worked for its residents. There were churches for most denominations. There was a policy script for these neighbourhoods; the government sought to break up the strongholds of working-class culture, with unemployment, crime, and anti-social behaviour.[5] The new urban layout of neighbourhoods such as Overvecht was to go hand-in-hand with the development of a new social structure, based on mixing people with different incomes and backgrounds. A variety of community centres catered to the wishes of young children, adolescents, and older people.

[1] F. Mulder, 'De overbodige klasse van Overvecht: "Iedereen heeft pijn in zijn rug"', *De Groene Amsterdammer*, 8 March 2017. Available at: http://bit.do/fJKiv (accessed 15 February 2020).

[2] See R. Venturi, D. Scott Brown, and S. Izenour, *Learning from Las Vegas: The Forgotten Symbolism of Architectural Form* (Cambridge, MA: MIT Press, 1977).

[3] Statistics Netherlands, *Kerncijfers wijken en buurten 2017*, 2017. Available at: http://bit.do/fJKiz (accessed 15 February 2020).

[4] R.E. Park, ed., *An Outline of the Principles of Sociology* (New York: Barnes & Noble, 1946), p. 252.

[5] G.H.L. Zeegers and L. de Jonge, 'De huidige toestand bij de wijkopbouw en de sociale problematiek er van', in *Enige aspecten van sociale wijkopbouw*, pp. 7–18 (The Hague: Staatsdrukkerij- en Uitgeverijbedrijf, 1955), p. 12.

↑ Housing associations own about two-third of the housing stock in Overvecht, and so a large majority of the dwellings in the neighbourhood are social housing (■)—most of them apartments in high-rise buildings. Owner-occupiers (■) often reside in rowhouses, as do some social tenants. Other rental properties (■) include for instance private rental housing and retirement homes.

Fig. 3.31 ↑ The northern part of Overvecht in the mid-1990s: a mix of high-rise, mid-rise, and single-family homes.

Fig. 3.32 → Two women looking over the spotless Oderdreef in the summer of 1967.

Fig. 3.33 (Next spread) Children on a tree planting day in Overvecht.

Geographically, Overvecht is well-positioned in the urban context. Utrecht's city centre is a fifteen-minute bike ride away. Furthermore, it is well connected by public transport (Overvecht has a railway station) and with direct access to the motorway between Utrecht, Amsterdam, and Schiphol Airport. The Maarsseveense Plassen [Lakes of Maarsseveen], a recreational area, is literally just across the road on the north-eastern edge of the neighbourhood.

Over the years, the neighbourhood has lost much of its strength and character. In the early 1990s the first signals of Overvecht's downward spiral became apparent. People who had higher disposable incomes started to move to (newly created) sub-urban settings, using the car for their daily commutes. In the early twenty-first century, Overvecht felt the competition of the new and nearby urbanization of Leidsche Rijn. Many chose to move to the thousands of new dwellings built in this district, where the majority of buildings were single-family homes, with some mid-rises in between.[6] Overvecht became the neighbourhood where people ended up that could not move or had nowhere (else) to go. Those who could take a next step on the urban ladder, which often implied moving out of Overvecht to better places elsewhere in the city, did so.

Over the past three decades, Utrecht's local government has sought to improve the social conditions in the neighbourhood with a wide array of programmes. One of these programmes, The Utrecht Challenge (De Utrechtse Opgave), was established in 2001 and planned for radical physical renewal, including the demolition of 9,500 social housing units, to be replaced by 3,000 new social housing units and 6,000 new owner-occupied homes.[7] But the global financial crisis of 2008 and beyond compromised the operations and achievements of this large-scale plan. Then there was a series of policy programmes that incorporated labour, health, education, safety, and poverty reduction into comprehensive social plans. And on top of these major programmes came a host of smaller ones, often also aimed at socioeconomic improvements. But benign as they were, they were not sufficient to resolve the multi-layered challenge for Overvecht and fully achieve the sort of social improvement that was aimed for.[8] And so Overvecht, which started as a neighbourhood for the future, has been tossed around from one local official to the next, all trying to come to grips with the sort of neighbourhood that we all recognize from elsewhere.

Overvecht as a *Pars Pro Toto* for Modernist High-Rise

Like so many high-rise neighbourhoods, Overvecht is characterized by the typical spatial modernist layout:

[6] City of Utrecht, *Analyse wonen en verhuizen in Overvecht* (Utrecht: City of Utrecht, 2015). Available at: http://bit.do/fJKiC (accessed 15 February 2020).

[7] City of Utrecht, Bo-Ex, Portaal, and Mitros, *Overvecht de Gagel vernieuwt: Sterke mensen, betere buurt: Concept gebiedsplan* (Utrecht: City of Utrecht, 2007). Available at: http://bit.do/fJKiE (accessed 15 February 2020); M. Hendriks, 'Ik zou nooit op de grond willen wonen', *Post Planjer*, 2009. Available at: http://bit.do/fJKiG (accessed 15 February 2020).

[8] See for instance: City of Utrecht, *Leren van de wijkaanpak: Van wijkaanpak naar buurtaanpak* (Utrecht: City of Utrecht, 2018). Available at: http://bit.do/fJKiK (accessed 15 February 2020); City of Utrecht, *Wijkactieprogramma 2017 Overvecht: Samen maken we Overvecht sneller vitaal* (Utrecht: City of Utrecht, 2017). Available at: http://bit.do/fJKiL (accessed 15 February 2020). A most recent shot at making Overvecht a better neighbourhood has been a programme called *Samen voor Overvecht (Together for Overvecht)*. See City of Utrecht, *Samen voor Overvecht* (Utrecht: City of Utrecht, 2019). Available at: http://bit.do/fJKiR (accessed 15 February 2020).

Fig. 3.34 ↗ Overvecht today: a paddling pool between the high-rises of the Ankaradreef and the Haifadreef.

Fig. 3.35 ↑ Ordering Vietnamese spring rolls on a cloudy day in Overvecht's shopping area.

Fig. 3.36 ↑ Aerial view of (part of) the Overvecht neighbourhood.

repetitive multiple-storey blocks, lots of space for car traffic, large chunks of 'undefined' green space, and the classic modernist separation of functions of little wards with distinct characteristics from larger chunks of land set aside for businesses—large-scale fitness centres; car repair and tyre shops; tile, carpet, and construction markets; and storage facilities catering for the surplus stuff that people accumulate over a lifetime. Shopping is done in shopping centres, the smaller ones dwindling, one bigger one surviving. In terms of sociability, the neighbourhood lacks the places between the home and the city. People have their own networks, for instance via family, religion, ethnic background. And Overvecht functions well as an arrival city. 'The neighbourhood is good to people who arrive here', says Marina Slijkerman, head of the Overvecht branch of the City of Utrecht. Moving into this neighbourhood, immigrants are most likely to find people who are in the same position as themselves. Also, Overvecht has become popular with students looking for low rents and with people who seek to purchase their first home in Utrecht's overheated housing market. Frankly, Overvecht is the only neighbourhood in the city that is still somewhat affordable.

Nowadays the 1960s chatter while feeling fruit at the grocery store can still be witnessed at the small local supermarkets— for instance, Meltem Plaza on the Theemsdreef, or Meknes in the very north of Overvecht. But one can also see the struggle to cope with the rigid morphology of the modernist buildings and layout. Lombok, a dense neighbourhood nearby, saw a large influx of migrant communities too. But whereas the central street in Lombok now offers a wide variety of shops and services, for all to see and explore, the current neighbourhood ecology of Overvecht makes it very difficult to allow such essential services in a way that creates a strong, collective public domain—the scale is too sheer, the density too low, the structure too vast.

We can read the story of Overvecht as a *pars pro toto* for similar neighbourhoods in Europe and North America. Modernist high-rise constellations, built to alleviate the serious post-war housing shortages, following a modernist take on both urban design and project development that was in vogue at the time. These areas often face the same cumulation of problems,[9] making it all the more relevant to think of ways to connect the energy transition to the other issues at play in such areas.

Social-ecological Renovation

We think Overvecht makes the case for what we would call a *social-ecological renovation*, which combines addressing the climate crisis and taking up the challenges that residents and local professionals face in the neighbourhood. While this may sound all too obvious, it is actually not at all easy to organize. In this chapter we detail the struggle of professionals and citizens of various walks of life to create an urban future for Overvecht, beginning with an unfortunate start of trying to make Overvecht a leading example, a neighbourhood for the future without any dependency on fossil fuel(s).

In 2017, the Mayor and Executive Board of the City of Utrecht put forward the northern section of Overvecht (again, Overvecht-Noord) as a testbed for the energy transition. It sounded like a noble idea: picking a disadvantaged neighbourhood to be the first to embark on an energy transition, making it an inspiration for other neighbourhoods to follow. The policy-making machine was started up. All residents of the neighbourhood received a letter from the municipality announcing the pending energy transition. Some of them had already heard about the decision through the national news or read it in the newspaper, days earlier. But being selected as a testbed did not feel like a prize at all, residents found. It rather felt like a burden; like they had to be the guinea pigs for a social experiment.[10]

Still, it was not that strange a decision if seen from the vantage point of the local government. With a left-leaning coalition in office, city hall wanted to be seen to be in the frontline of the greening of the city. Policymakers had pointed out that a significant part of the neighbourhood's gas network had aged and required replacement. Moreover, housing associations owned about two-third of the housing stock; their predominant homeownership in the neighbourhood would make it easier to coordinate the transition. And the government thought there would be opportunities to combine the technical operation with a socioeconomic

[9] See for instance Saunders, *Arrival City*, 2012; Crimson Historians & Urbanists, *A City of Comings and Goings* (Rotterdam: nai010, 2019).

[10] F. Mulder, 'Utrechtse wijk moet van het gas af: "Niet iets wat je even uitrolt"', *De Groene Amsterdammer*, 28 August 2019. Available at: http://bit.do/fJKiV (accessed 15 February 2020); H. van de Wiel, '"Aardgasvrij wordt ons door de strot geduwd"', *Tijdschrift voor Sociale Vraagstukken*, 21 December 2018. Available at: http://bit.do/fJKiX (accessed 15 February 2020).

operation in the area. Yet the announcement met with rebounding sentiments of anger and anxiety from residents, particularly from owners of the 1,300 owner-occupied homes in Overvecht-Noord.[11]

Bastiaan Staffhorst works for Mitros, a local housing association. He states: 'Overvecht is indeed at the lower end of the city's housing market. And then *that* is where you tell homeowners that you are going to cut them off and request them to invest 30,000 euros in their homes?' And while Peter Hulshof, an active Overvecht resident, understands the ambition, he also says: 'You have to be cognizant of the playing field. This is the city's poorest neighbourhood, and there is a serious risk of magnifying the divide between the rich and the poor.' Els Wegdam, who is a long-term resident and chairs the Neighbourhood Platform, uses stronger words: 'As pioneers we are bound to pay too much for this operation. And others would take benefit from the burden that we would be bearing.'

First Lessons

What we can learn from Overvecht is how easy it is to slip into what we call the *objectification* of a neighbourhood: the area is regarded according to its properties, and solutions are defined accordingly. The relationship of the government to the neighbourhood becomes one of statistical analysis, optimization, and decision making, followed by 'professional communication' to organize legitimacy. To a certain extent that is how policymakers are trained, of course. Yet it is also a case of modernist slippage. It overlooks the sensitivities of citizens and mostly tends to forget consulting those government workers that have first-hand knowledge of the neighbourhood. Michael Lipsky famously called them 'street-level bureaucrats'.[12]

In the age of climate crisis, neighbourhoods require updates on their energy systems, taking away fossil fuels for heating and cooking, and insulating homes to save energy. Yet while this may be a focal point for the general public, it is not the first problem on the list of people living in Overvecht, or of those people working in and for the neighbourhood on a daily basis. Neighbourhood professionals, such as community workers, or professionals working for housing associations, would characteristically point to the accumulation of problems happening behind doors, from poor health situations to unemployment, from crime and drugs to bad or no education at all.[13]

The first step toward a strategy of social-ecological renovation came in late 2018 when a dedicated project team started a consultation process to come to a transition plan. That was also when a

[11] DUIC, 'Wie betaalt de rekening voor proefwijk gasvrij Overvecht-Noord?', *DUIC*, 25 June 2018. Available at: http://bit.do/fJKi2 (accessed 15 February 2020); C. Huisman, 'Overvecht gasvrij? Dat gaat de bewoners een beetje te snel', *de Volkskrant*, 2 May 2018. Available at: http://bit.do/fJKi3 (accessed 15 February 2020); RTV Utrecht, 'Aardgasvrije huizen: Bewoners Overvecht-Noord vrezen gepeperde rekening', *RTV Utrecht*, 28 November 2017. Available at: http://bit.do/fJKi4 (accessed 15 February 2020); RTV Utrecht, 'Petitie tegen proef aardgasvrij Overvecht', *RTV Utrecht*, 8 February 2018. Available at: http://bit.do/fJKi6 (accessed 15 February 2020); A. Schouten, 'Milieuwethouder Van Hooijdonk vindt Overvecht op haar weg richting "aardgasvrij Utrecht"', *Algemeen Dagblad*, 6 November 2018. Available at: http://bit.do/fJKi7 (accessed 13 January 2020); I. Tasseron and P. Knieriem, 'Aardgasvrij wonen is duur, maar er is geen ontkomen aan', *RTV Utrecht*, 7 November 2018. Available at: http://bit.do/fJKi8 (accessed 15 February 2020).

[12] M. Lipsky, *Street-Level Bureaucracy: Dilemmas of the Individual in Public Services* (New York, NY: Russell Sage Foundation, 2010); cf. B. Zacka, *When the State Meets the Street: Public Service and Moral Agency* (Cambridge, MA: Harvard University Press, 2017).

series of public participation events with homeowners, 'neighbour-hood conversations' as the project team labelled them, started and went on throughout 2019. These conversations, as well as an appoint-ed consultative group of homeowners, provided input for the transi-tion plan. The municipality argued that the operation had to be both affordable and feasible for residents. The delivery of the transition plan in the fall of 2019 marked the end of a first phase in the process toward taking Overvecht-Noord off the natural-gas grid.[14] This had been a phase of picking up people's perspectives and opinions, fol-lowing a participation model that was a mixture between informing and consulting. Mark Elbers—hired to spearhead the project team on behalf of the municipality, housing associations, energy network oper-ator Stedin, and energy cooperative Energie-U—says that the parti-cipation revolved around two technical questions: (1) which heating systems exist? And (2) what criteria should be applied when choosing a new heating system for the neighbourhood? Here we see the second point of slippage: while opening up to the citizenry through a consul-tation process, the government still follows siloed bureaucratic lines—in this case prioritizing the technical part of the job.

There is always a risk in connecting different spheres of responsibilities; making a plea for an 'integrated' approach may end up in numbing complexity and never-ending discussions that do not lead to a feasible plan. That rationale was also behind the choice to keep Overvecht-Noord's energy transition separate from other 'siloes', but as the initial outburst of opposition had slowed down in 2019, a sec-tor-based approach to urban sustainability began to shine through. 'We have to be honest to the residents: first and foremost, our assignment is to take their homes off the natural-gas grid', Mark Elbers explains. He is the first to admit that many residents already have plenty of other things to worry about at home, and that it would make sense to con-nect to those other concerns. But he also admits that, at this stage, he and his team do not have a concrete plan for making such connections.

Sometimes a sector-based approach can work magically. For instance, when it comes to insulation. Housing associations do this as part of renovating their buildings in Overvecht, and some of them experiment with new methods of making buildings more sustainable.[15] Climate-proofing is not much of a priority to them, says Bastiaan Staffhorst at Mitros: 'We are just trying to improve our portfolio, an operation which now just happens to include replacing gas cookers with induction ones—and that's that.' But while this is expedient in a situation where a housing association can bear the costs and has the organizational power, it is not so obvious with individual homeowners. Then an energetic transition is probably too narrow a policy focus for people to feel tempted to engage in it. And so, the municipality mainly continues to try to persuade

[13] Y. Tieleman, 'Onderwereld voelt zich iets te goed thuis in Overvecht', *Algemeen Dagblad*, 26 May 2017. Available at: http://bit.do/fJKi9 (accessed 15 February 2020).

[14] City of Utrecht, Stedin, Mitros, Bo-Ex, Portaal, Eneco, & Energie-U, *Transitieplan Overvecht-Noord aardgasvrij* (Utrecht: City of Utrecht, 2019). Available at: http://bit.do/fJKja (accessed 15 February 2020).

[15] CorporatieGids Magazine, 'Bo-Ex: Durf te experimenteren bij verduurzamingsopgave', *CorporatieGids Magazine* no. 2, 2018, pp. 29–31. Available at: http://bit.do/fJKjc (accessed 15 February 2020).

residents and stakeholders to come along and get something done on the energy transition, but perhaps too much harm has been done by setting off on the wrong foot with the testbed announcement of 2017.

The Future of Overvecht

In the philosophy underlying this book, with its emphasis on neighbourhood ecologies connecting the ecological and the social dimensions, we must try and establish the link between the need to on the one hand act on the energy transition and on the other the wish to address issues of affordability and inclusiveness, and to also try to make the neighbourhood a more pleasant place to live in. But how to do that? Based on inspiring examples of activities and events that are not connected to the energy transition, and that we discussed with people living or working in Overvecht, we distinguish four strategies as alternatives to a sector-oriented approach: (1) an area-based approach, (2) a co-benefit approach, (3) a 'clear goals, open solutions' approach, and (4) a placemaking strategy.

An Area-Based Approach What seems a logical step to consider here is to move away from a reactive, disjointed, and siloed approach to address problem and crises, towards an area-based approach in which solutions are sought by approaching sets of problems as interrelated questions. 'I once hoped that we would be able to incorporate the energy transition into an overarching model for the transformation of Overvecht. But so far I have not observed anything like it.' Sander Willemsen is the director of Energie-U, a local energy cooperative that aspires to promote, organize, and safeguard the proliferation of sustainable energy in people's homes. Difficult questions are put aside, he says.

> *What's in it for the neighbourhood, really? Do people get a better neighbourhood, better homes, better lives, by making this energy transition? We are avoiding this conversation. And here we are dearly missing the power of imagination. We are not able to go beyond discussing how to reduce our carbon emissions.*

The versatility of problems tends to be reduced.
An interesting experiment takes place at the Vulcanusdreef. Here, once more, we saw that the true problem for the housing associations active in Overvecht is not the energy transformation. It is the lack of control over some housing estates. The Vulcanusdreef is tucked away in the far eastern tip of Overvecht, where a building block derailed over the course of several years. It had initially been designed to host the elderly, but other residents gradually moved in and the complex spiralled out of control, with drugs trading and production, and sheltering criminals. And yet people at Mitros, the housing association owning the real estate, did not have a clue about what was going on. They provided maintenance services

and the building looked spic and span because it had just been reno-vated. Staff at the housing association were not aware that police of-ficers were called out there daily, for instance, to prevent neighbourly disputes from escalating. Neither was the health care provider, which had clients in this area. Everyone was only seeing their piece of the puzzle—real estate, security, or care—instead of the bigger picture.

The layered cake of problems only became clear when the housing association, the police department, and the health care provider had an interdisciplinary conversation. Together they opted for an area-based, problem-oriented approach. Focusing on the block, they saw the interconnections, as well as the ways to improve the cir-cumstances in and around the building. Drug-dealing residents were taken out and young, first-time renters replaced them and brought a new vibe to the block.

This area-based approach can work, also because it leads to tangible results. 'I like to call it a social renovation', says Reijnder Jan Spits. He is a manager at Portaal, a housing association that owns about 4,000 units in Overvecht—all in high-rise and mid-rise apartment blocks. Portaal tries to improve the social sustainabil-ity of the neighbourhood by bringing into the social housing blocks people that are, in some respects, 'stronger' than most tenants who live there. As Spits explains the rationale, he invites us to think of a resident who has been living in Overvecht since the 1960s. On the left of his apartment a Syrian family moves in—they do not speak each other's language. On the other side, a mentally ill person, someone with a disturbed sleep pattern, becomes his new neighbour. Spits asks us a rhetorical question: 'Can we expect this long-term resident to take his new neighbours by the hand and help them build a future in the neighbourhood? Aren't we demanding a little too much from an underprivileged community?' His take is that tenants with a different background may be of more help in welcoming and assisting the ex-cluded, the vulnerable, and the reintegrated. Portaal started allocating some of its dwellings to different people.[16] Ex-drug addicts are now sharing a block with young, ambitious people who provide coaching in language, household administration, or labour market opportunities.

A Co-Benefit Approach The inclination of policymakers to stick to a sectoral agenda is understandable; within their sector, they have a higher degree of control. Yet, as we pointed out above, a sectoral approach quickly touches upon its limits, in particular in neighbour-hoods like Overvecht. When asked about the reasons for still sticking to a sector-based approach, people often refer to the lack of results that come with its opposite, an integrated approach. Yet this leaves out a viable second route: a co-benefit approach. This approach entails 'frontloading' a policy commitment (say, 'Overvecht must be CO_2 neutral in 2030'), putting that public goal above the discussion, and then focus-ing entirely on trying to create co-benefits. Unlike an

[16] DUIC, 'Goede buur' gezocht voor woningen aan de Bangkokdreef van Portaal', *DUIC*, 18 April 2019. Available at: http://bit.do/fJKjr (accessed 15 February 2020).

Fig. 3.37 ↑ Children sitting atop a public ping-pong table.

integrated approach, the priority area is clear. But the orientation for governance is to find strong co-benefits.

Overvecht provides opportunities for co-benefits. It has already seen several projects that embrace this approach. In Bouw=Wouw (Construction=Cool), contractors and housing associations have teamed up with schools to reach out to youth in Overvecht and promote working in the construction sector. The initiative has led housing associations to hire young locals in the operation of renovating their portfolio in Overvecht. It also has a nice ring to it seen from the energy transition that lies ahead: making arrangements with employers that would enable youth living in Overvecht to contribute to the future of their very own community by installing solar panels, wall insulation, or heat pumps in their blocks.

Another example of the co-benefit approach is the 2016 initiative of Plan Einstein. It organized social events—meals, sports, language cafés—to help refugees, often Syrians, build a future in the arrival city, bringing them in touch with residents and businesses. Here, the agenda of receiving refugees was put above the discussion, and co-benefits were found in building opportunities for refugees and Overvecht locals to learn from and be of help to one another, with eyes on education and personal development.

And then there is Project O, a network organization founded in 2019 and one of the latest shots at achieving co-benefits. In it, Arjen van Ree, a local entrepreneur who got inspired by Plan Einstein, aspires to extend the perspective of education and talent development, linking it to the challenges that the neighbourhood is facing. 'Overvecht's imminent energy transition opens doors to a wide range of community benefits', says Van Ree. One of his ideas is

Fig. 3.38 ↑ Preparing a community meal of Brussels sprouts.

Fig. 3.39 → An Overvecht resident wearing a neighbourhood t-shirt.

to appoint Overvecht locals from diverse cultural backgrounds as so-called 'energy ambassadors', and to assign them the task of reaching out to as many residents as possible to exchange information, ideas, and concerns. He emphasizes the great value this strategy could have for community building, awareness, and commitment.

In Overvecht there is a strong tradition of networking and collaborating between residents on the one hand and entrepreneurs and public officials on the other. The social infrastructure of the neighbourhood is one of myriad and often overlapping networks.[17] Every Saturday, residents meet up at a local catering project for a free meal, cooked with ingredients donated by grocery stores and bakeries. The project is called Buurtbuik—Dutch for 'neighbourhood belly'. Three community centres provide space for gatherings of all kinds. And three dedicated grassroots organizations defend and promote the interests of residents: the Platform for Residents, founded in 1997 in response to the increasing problems in the area; the Neighbourhood Platform, an active group of residents, shop owners, school teachers, and entrepreneurs; and Echt Overvecht [Real Overvecht], an association that seeks to improve Overvecht's image and publishes a quarterly magazine about the neighbourhood. A co-benefit approach could thrive on this existing social infrastructure.

A 'Clear Goals, Open Solutions' Approach How networks are designed affects the dynamics of how problems are approached and resolved. A unidirectional design, from policy to practice, serves the bureaucratic system: it contains clear performance objectives and accountability lines between the actors involved, and the making of a transition plan for Overvecht-Noord fits that description. But what if the best ideas are not invented in city hall but somewhere else, that is, 'on the ground'? In those cases, a 'clear goals, open solutions' strategy is worth considering. Using this approach means that the government is crystal clear about its goals, but stimulates others to come up with proposals. Rather than seeing society as an object, it is based on the idea of society as a subject, and it aims at unlocking societal energy. Promising solutions are often found by others, and then the smartest strategy might be to hop on and eventually chip in—if it suits your agenda.

'The energy transition is not a technical issue, it is a social process.' Gerbert Hengelaar is clear about his agenda. The City of Utrecht would love to pre-select and 'roll out' tech solutions as soon as possible, but he and his neighbours have a different ambition. They established a community initiative with 120

[17] Z. Seghrouchni, 'Dit is Bob Scherrenberg, ontwikkelaar van de veerkrachtige stad', *Post Planjer*, 1 May 2016. Available at: http://bit.do/fJKjs (accessed 15 February 2020).

households and wrote a manifesto about designing a way forward in the energy transition in their streets in the western part of Overvecht.[18] Here, we see a group of owner-occupiers who can find the time to think along with the government. Hengelaar nuances the earlier images of the reluctant attitude among Overvecht's residents regarding the energy transition: not everyone considers himself or herself a victim or a 'guinea pig'. Hengelaar's neighbours are excited about looking for a new energy future for their communities. And while exploring that future they experience a feeling of coming closer to one another:

> *It really makes us feel proud to be part of this neighbourhood. It is so much more than tackling the single challenge of an energy transition. With this strategy, we are connecting people more effectively, by convening more open conversations about what is important and how to organize things.*

It is not a walk in the park. In evening hours and weekends, all voluntarily, Hengelaar and his partners schedule, chair, and process numerous meetings, large and small, formal and informal. They designed a voting scheme for go-no-go moments in their search for a widely supported strategy towards a solution. Hengelaar: 'For an energy transition you probably have no choice but to go beyond a conventional level of consultation, especially at this early, often uncertain stage.' He still is surprised by the wealth of human capital that came to the surface once neighbours started organizing themselves: energy experts, housing professionals, long-term residents. This type of initiative could have a bigger effect on Overvecht. Key for governments is to make sure that such initiatives have easy access to technical, financial, and legal expertise.

There is positive energy and a sense of ownership about the civil initiative that has yet to emerge, about the municipality's top-down plan that was presented in 2017. And so, media exposure for the benign alternative has grown. Hengelaar is hardly able to keep up with press invitations, so he crams talks about his brainchild into his daily half-hour car commutes between Amsterdam and Utrecht. Before hanging up after our phone call, he concludes: 'We should probably cherish our civil society a little more and consider it a valuable asset in transitions.'

A Placemaking Approach Overvecht might be a complex neighbourhood, but still, developers are interested in the area. While some developers opt for the certainties of *tabula rasa* locations or greenfield development, others are both interested and successful in redeveloping existing urban areas. This requires a different approach, as potential buyers themselves will have to buy property and live there. This is what placemaking is about. It is somewhat controversial in circles of urban sociologists; some argue that placemaking is a stepping stone to gentrification, driving out current residents to be replaced by

[18] Nieuwe Energie voor de Vechtzoom, *Buurtmanifest Nieuwe Energie voor de Vechtzoom*, 2019. Available at: http://bit.do/fJKjD (accessed 15 February 2020).

more affluent others. However, in many cases, such as in Regent Park but potentially also in Overvecht, it is or can be envisaged as 'adding' people and real estate to the existing neighbourhood. Sure, critics could then still argue that this will lead to a cultural form of gentrification, as posh services (laundry, French bakery, high-end restaurant) replace existing services catering for people with low incomes. But this is not necessarily the case. Placemaking can work to keep a mix of functions intact or even improve it.

Peter van der Gugten is an experienced redeveloper of urban areas. He once headed a housing association, and his discourse is full of social consciousness. 'You have to delve deeply into what is happening in a neighbourhood, what is bothering residents, and what is driving them, before even beginning to think of an intervention of any kind.' Van der Gugten advocates an almost cultural approach towards neighbourhood building. On behalf of Heijmans, a Dutch project development firm, he directed some of the largest urban regeneration programmes in the Netherlands in the past couple of decades—all to critical acclaim. 'If you start with an in-depth exercise, you are bound to find people who have the energy to create or build something special', Van der Gugten says. There is no need to discuss with residents the nitty-gritty or technicalities of specific solutions. But there has to be a willingness on the part of a 'quartermaster', whether it is a public commissioner or a private developer, to hear about what a neighbourhood or community means to its people, what people value, and what they miss. No matter how mundane their concerns are or how irrelevant their grievances may seem, this is how you build up an environment of trust, acknowledgement, and ownership among residents. 'And in this environment, you will hear what is important to bear in mind when building a new future for people. This is where they will tell you stories about their cultures, their struggles, their aspirations.'

Placemaking is a strategy in which the energy transition would be encapsulated in making good new places that show that there are alternative futures for Overvecht. The future of Overvecht then is about (re)building a neighbourhood. 'We get the issue of sustainability, really, we do', says developer Van der Gugten. 'But what we often don't seem to deliver on in the neighbourhoods we build is that people feel at home, feel like they matter, feel that we built a place for them.' To him, it remains difficult to nail the wide range of issues that are key to building good neighbourhoods. There is no mathematical formula or law of physics, but he will say that drivers should be in the social domain—not in the domain of an energy transition. Good neighbourhoods improve public health and help resolve crime problems. Placemaking in the sense presented above, which is about creating environments in which a new, enhanced mix of functions emerges and maybe a more diverse community starts to see a future in the neighbourhood, could be a promising strategy for Overvecht.

If Overvecht is to become an imaginary of turning modernist post-war settlements into well-functioning urban neighbourhoods, adding new building stock seems unavoidable. Looking at its spatial form, that is precisely where the potential of modernist neighbourhoods lies, with their surpluses of unused space and low floor space indices. It seems just as inevitable to selectively demolish building stock. The modernist structures are often not adaptive enough to host the sort of urban designs that would allow for a new, working neighbourhood ecology to really take off.[19]

'In the beginning, it's all about small injections', Van der Gugten replies when we ask how he catalyzes change. 'Small initiatives in the neighbourhood, in strategic places. Close to people's lives, easy to recognize.' Wherever change is occurring—a redesigned street, a retrofitted square, a new bistro or festival—you can experience hope or a new future: someone has been investing in your neighbourhood. Yet one also needs to show a long-term dedication to social-ecological renovation. Of course, there is a phase of pioneering and experimenting, and it is key to getting things going. But Van der Gugten insists on sustainable commitments to a neighbourhood for it to stay healthy, vibrant, and pleasant in the long run; it is about the long-term operation of a neighbourhood. Continuity, or viability if you will, requires a particular mode of ongoing attention and governance.

The Governance of Change

The social-ecological renovation of modernist neighbourhoods that are dominated by high-rise is mindbogglingly complex. Yet speaking to the people living in and working on Overvecht, we can unravel a pattern. It is crucial to dare to engage, be on the ground, listen, ask questions, allow trust to build up. Some fifty years ago, as the Netherlands started a large-scale national programme of urban renewal ('stadsvernieuwing' in Dutch), some lessons were learned that now still are of use. Be *in* the neighbourhood with a project team that has true power; allow yourself to learn, so redevelop piecemeal, block by block; and always be clear about a conflict resolution mechanism: which body can decide if interests do not align? Crucial was the commitment to work in the neighbourhood; civil servants and active citizens were physically present, talked, and developed plans based on knowledge of what was going on.

Distance, not being in the neighbourhood, leads to all sorts of mechanisms that, when they come out, infuriate residents. Take the language as an example. The higher up the administrative ranks, the more people use euphemisms to address the conditions. They talk about 'vulnerable neighbourhoods' in which people live with 'a distance to the labour market', have 'a backpack' (shorthand for a social indication), or make 'wrong lifestyle choices' (eating fish and chips, smoking). But with this language comes a growing distance to the actual world of the residents of Overvecht. In one instance during our research, a high-ranked government official found himself lost in the neighbourhood, asking us for directions.

[19] R. Cazander, 'Overvecht verliest slechts één tienhoogflat', *Algemeen Dagblad*, 6 October 2016. Available at: http://bit.do/fJKjG (accessed 15 February 2020); M. Doodeman, 'BPD en Mitros willen Utrechtse corporatieflats slopen en dure woningen terugbouwen', *Cobouw*, 21 May 2019. Available at: http://bit.do/fJKjJ (accessed 15 February 2020); DUIC, 'Plan voor sloop sociale huurwoningen: Overvecht voor huur- en koopwoningen', *DUIC*, 20 May 2019. Available at: http://bit.do/fJKjL (accessed 15 February 2020).

Overvecht reveals the risks of treating a neighbourhood as an object. 'It' emits too much CO_2 and needs to be regulated. While understandable in light of the climate crisis and the need to reach national goals, we think this strategy is not going to succeed in complex neighbourhoods. To be sure, a sector-based approach can work in some parts, particularly in reaching sectoral goals like reducing CO_2 emissions. In cases where the ownership is collective and measures are routinely 'added' to the general maintenance of real estate, such as in the case of housing associations, a straightforward strategy can produce great results. But neighbourhoods such as Overvecht call for a much broader approach: a 'social-ecological renovation'. Look for synergies and you will see the need to address the climate issue as an entry point for a broader attempt to improve the neighbourhood.

Interestingly, Overvecht shows the potential starting points for alternative approaches. What we see is that they all require both willingness and ability to engage with the neighbourhood, its people, whether residents or neighbourhood professionals and its places. This requires a cultural turnaround, an approach in which societal voices are heard by the government. Overvecht reveals that even in the most difficult of neighbourhoods there are the elements of a neighbourhood ecology to relate to. But these do not feature in statistics. They require a more anthropological eye and ear, an appreciation for the street.

Fig. 3.40 ↓ Neighbourhood arrangement of Overvecht.

DISCOURSE	— Making an energy transition in an underprivileged community.
ACTORS	— Several institutions have established a joint project team that is dedicated to planning the energy transition of Overvecht-Noord; — Housing associations take up the task of renovating their portfolio, making it more sustainable; — Owner-occupiers are grouping up in an initiative and choose their own adventure in the energy transition; — Developers are looking for opportunities to intervene in Overvecht.
RESOURCES	— Generally siloed approach to funding change in the neighbourhood with public sector money; — Housing associations pay sustainability measures out of their own pockets; homeowners are expected to pay for the energy transition themselves, as long as it is feasible and affordable.
RULES	— Rules for the energy transition in Overvecht-Noord are still in the making.

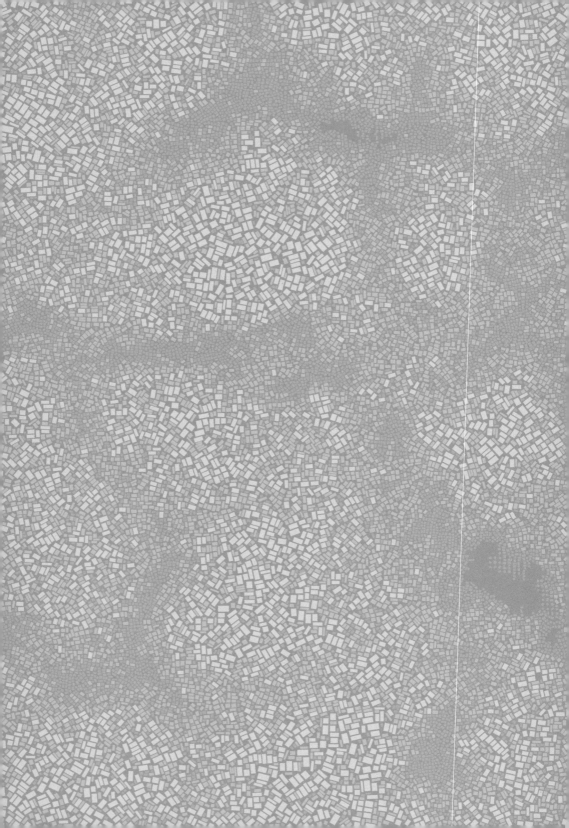

4   The Neighbourhood as Modest Imaginary

This book originates from an urge to address the vast ecological crisis Earth is facing; if we want to prevent blowing the fuses of our planet, urbanization needs to change tack. As we argued in the introductory essay, neighbourhoods are a critical scale to do so. They are small enough to be tangible yet big enough to make a difference. Moreover, we argued that we should hark back to the rich history of urbanism that has helped us to both understand and shape our cities. A resulting premise is that the ecological can and should never be seen apart from the social. District heating, reducing the space reserved for cars while introducing new forms of mobility, having shops and other amenities in the vicinity of your home, all are to be seen in connection to how such actions influence existing social networks, allow for, or stand in the way of, new social networks and new urban lifestyles. Likewise, the city itself affects sustainability: the existing physical fabric of a neighbourhood influences how we can or should think about taking on the sustainability challenge, as the experience with modernist neighbourhoods makes clear.

For all its analytical effort, this book hopes to inspire and enthuse. As we said in the preface, we deliberately stay clear of providing new recipes in a 'cookbook' style; that would be modernism all over again. The book is much more about appreciation of the value of the neighbourhood as the focus of our attention, and the intricacies of trying to preserve and enhance the qualities of well-functioning neighbourhoods. Shaping our future neighbourhoods requires, above all, a sensitivity to context and the craft of situated judgement. In short, this book attempts to provide ideas on what could be, not about what should be.[1] We put forward the neighbourhood as a modest imaginary: a set of ideas and examples that could help to shape neighbourhoods of the future, while the actual work—the thinking, the doing, the committing—has to be done by local actors. In this sense, our insistence on the importance of the level of the neighbourhood is also a statement on how we think that the sustainability challenge can be connected to an open and democratic process of choosing the futures we want.

In this book, we coined two concepts to further the research on neighbourhoods: neighbourhood ecology and neighbourhood arrangements. The former was introduced to illuminate the importance of the connection between the physical and the social structure of a neighbourhood. It is our conceptual translation of ecological urbanism, a form of urbanism of which the ecological dimension is an intrinsic part, not an add-on. The concept of the neighbourhood arrangement was introduced to bridge the gap between the ideal of a new neighbourhood ecology and the actual practice of getting there. It is the stabilization of actors, discourses, rules, and resources that are needed to approach the desired 'ecology'. We also added a normative dimension to it. A 'good' neighbourhood arrangement is one in which (most) actors have a long-term commitment ('skin

[1] H. Couclelis, '"Where Has the Future Gone?" Rethinking the Role of Integrated Land-use Models in Spatial Planning', *Environment and Planning A* 37, no. 8 (2005), pp. 1353–1371.

in the neighbourhood'); there is a strong narrative (i.e. discourse) that activates and mobilizes people; the rules are simple, in the sense that they are stringent on the goals yet leave room for trying out different solutions; and financial resources are created, captured, and circulated in the neighbourhood itself as much as possible. Drawing on the notions of neighbourhood ecology and neighbourhood arrangement, we tease out nine lessons based on our in-depth cases (Bo01, Regent Park, and Overvecht) and the findings of the research we presented in the thirteen shorter vignettes.

1. Develop Neighbourhoods Beyond the Car

One of the best ways to improve on both the social and ecological qualities of the city is to reconnect functions on a much lower scale. The modern city was regional, but an ecological urbanism as we see it will provide much more functions and amenities on the neighbourhood scale. Portland, Oregon, adopted the principle of a 'twenty-minute neighbourhood' where all functions besides work can be reached in a twenty-minute walk or bike ride. Interestingly, this results in a neighbourhood ecology that bears resemblances to the city as it existed before the automobile entered the stage. A city where pedestrians, boats, horses, and later bicycles got people around. Because these means of transportation were relatively slow, people lived close to each other with almost all their needs (shopping, trading, culture) nearby. Beside time gains, such an approach will relieve cities from the grip of the (privately owned) car, freeing up an enormous amount of space, both from roads and parking spots. This truly restructures the urban, allowing for sociable public space, parks that also function as water retention areas, and bicycle highways with good air quality. It is not just imagination. In our inquiry we found several neighbourhoods that function well while providing a very limited role for (private) automobiles. These include GWL in Amsterdam, Vauban in Freiburg, and Hunziker Areal in Zurich.

Importantly, it is not only the car that can connect neighbourhoods to the wider urban fabric; collective forms of (rail) transport have an important role to play. The concept of Transit-Oriented Development (TOD) envisions how neighbourhoods close to transit hubs can be both 'nodes' in a wider network and 'places' where people dwell and interact.[2] Nordhavn in Copenhagen, for example, is built along a light rail track that takes residents quickly to other parts of the city; unlike in Bo01, the construction of the public transit system started well before the development was complete. This allowed residents to adapt their lifestyles, organizing themselves around non-motorized means of transportation right from the moment they started living in their new neighbourhood. It then leads to reinstating and materializing a version of Walter Christaller's well-known central place theory, which prescribes that most daily needs such as shopping, day-care, and recreation are available in the neighbourhood. Simultaneously, a public transit system ensures that higher-order services elsewhere in the city are also within easy reach, allowing urbanites to go to musicals, football matches or other live events, visit a museum, or join a demonstration.

2. Let 'Smart' Work for Your Neighbourhood Ecology

'Smart' technology is knocking on urban's door. This is not per se bad, but not per se good either. It depends on how we integrate it in our daily lives. Smart applications should always be judged on their contribution to the functioning of cities or neighbourhoods. Yet once the twenty-minute neighbourhood settles in our minds, it helps focus on what we want new digital technologies to help achieve. The Finish example of Kalasatama shows how apps can potentially save residents time and plan their days more efficiently. On a larger scale, using smart technology can help to strengthen public transit solutions, such as light trail, trams, and trains. This potentially allows people to use the wider, more efficient daily urban system that incurs less congestion and pollution. Yet, 'smart' can also undercut the social essentials of neighbourhood life. Online shopping currently undercuts the 'nodes' in many neighbourhoods. Many typical shopping streets are emptying out because of the availability of cheap online alternatives while all the delivery vans create new traffic in our streets. Moreover, our vignette of Villiers Island briefly touches upon the Quayside development in the Toronto waterfront. Here, Sidewalk Labs (a subsidiary of Alphabet, Google's mother company) won the bid and is leading the development of a neighbourhood of five hectares. At first glance, the plans adhere to much of the principles of a good neighbourhood ecology as outlined in this book: Quayside is to become a dense, diverse, and energy-neutral new part of Toronto. Still, Sidewalk Labs has been receiving a lot of criticism. The public scepticism is mostly about the proposed digitalization and concomitant use of data. In a 'smart' neighbourhood, new issues arise: how will moral values like privacy, autonomy, and accessibility be safeguarded if a neighbourhood is increasingly steered by a digital platform? Is urban anonymity still possible in a neighbourhood with camera surveillance, digital check-ins, and apps that help you save an hour a day? Furthermore, we suggest that this seemingly small-scale development should be understood as a real-life 'urban lab' which will have consequences for the development of the much larger waterfront, and, beyond that, as an export product of a new style of urban development for the decades to come. Reasons enough to very carefully assess how smart technologies are employed in this context.

Issues of 'surveillance capitalism'[3] are to be debated at higher political levels, but the history of urban social movements shows that bottom-up protests have played a significant role in correcting grand modernist schemes of urban renewal, and with a worldwide effect. So, once again, neighbourhoods could be in the

(2) L. Bertolini, 'Spatial Development Patterns and Public Transport: The Application of an analytical Model in the Netherlands', *Planning Practice and Research* 14, no. 2 (1999), pp. 199–210.

frontline, showing alternative employments of smart technologies that do enhance the ecology of the local neighbourhood. The sort of interaction that we saw in the Utrecht neighbourhood of Lombok, where a local entrepreneur introduced a smart grid that really worked for the neighbourhood, is something that will not be imagined at the R&D desks of the big tech firms. This is where innovative neighbourhoods can really make a difference. Planners thus need to reinvent neighbourhood arrangements that make digitalization work for their neighbourhood ecology. Regarding resources, the profits of platform innovations such as accommodation platforms (e.g. Airbnb) could largely flow back to the neighbourhood. Moreover, simple rules could work here as well (see more on these in our seventh lesson), for example by limiting the number of stays by tourists or by capping vehicle miles travelled by ride-sourcing companies and stipulating that they should also provide mobility to commercially less interesting groups.

3. From Tabula Rasa to Tabula Scripta

In a taut piece on the blog *Failed Architecture*, Mark Minkjan critiqued contemporary architects for how they use visualizations.[4] Renderings show a biased and often misleading picture of urban futures, devoid of struggle and laden with technological fixes. In our search for inspiring neighbourhoods for the future, we stumbled upon a similar issue. The research for this book included an online inquiry into neighbourhoods with high sustainability ambitions. We found a wealth of visualizations of neighbourhoods-yet-to-be-built; all looking green and pleasant, and all with slick architecture. Yet, none of the images commented on the complexities and ambiguities involved in the development of a new neighbourhood. Just as with Le Corbusier and his contemporaries decades earlier, these were neighbourhoods born on the (digital) drawing table. It proved much harder to find *existing* inspiring and ambitious neighbourhoods, where people live, hang out, get by on a daily basis, and sort of know each other.

The in-depth analyses of Bo01, Regent Park, and Overvecht provided us with a very different picture. More nuanced, for sure; Bo01 turned out to not quite be the ecotopia we initially envisioned it to be. Its dwellers were as addicted to the car and electric appliances as people from neighbourhoods we do not read about in architecture magazines. Moreover, Overvecht taught us how important it is to not try and build a future on what is new and seemingly innovative but to investigate what is already there and then try to think how to change tack and improve the neighbourhood. The vast majority of neighbourhoods of the future in the Global North will not be built on greenfield land; they will be adaptations to the existing social and physical fabric. Tabula scripta rather than tabula rasa.[5] This requires a different way of looking, a different epistemological entry point. The community of scholars and planners need to learn to

(3) S. Zuboff, *The Age of Surveillance Capitalism: The Fight for a Human Future at the New Frontier of Power* (New York, NY: PublicAffairs, 2019).

(4) M. Minkjan, 'What This MVRDV Rendering Says about Architecture and the Media', *Failed Architecture*, 15 February 2016. Available at: http://bit.do/fJ4tF (accessed 20 February 2020).

see and appreciate the 'evolutionary potential' of present neighbour-hoods.[6] Getting to know a neighbourhood requires talking to people. This is about a genuine interest to understand a neighbourhood, about spending time there and being open to serendipity. As planner Trevor Graham remarked about his work in Augustenborg, Malmö, there is value in spending daytime shifts sitting on a bench at a bus stop, talking to people about whatever is going on in their lives. This will not be effortless at all. It will consume time, but in the end, it will be much more rewarding.

4. Don't Just Build Dwellings; Create Better Neighbourhoods Instead

We found that increasing the density of cities can, if done well, improve a neighbourhood ecology. Moreover, researchers of urban sustain-ability have argued that increasing density is inevitable to stay within planetary limits. As we noted above, the current trend in urbanization is the opposite: cities *de-densify* at a rate of two percent a year.[7]

Yet in Regent Park the density was increased dramati-cally, adding dwellings for higher-income groups while guaranteeing the right of return of the original residents of the social housing pro-jects. It is an interesting intervention in a context where adding condo-miniums to existing neighbourhoods is observed with suspicion, often invoking the risk of 'gentrification'. The argument is often that original inhabitants are driven out. That was not the case in Regent Park. We think that densification, combined with the effort to diversify deprived neighbourhoods, makes sense. The prime reason is that more diversity of income and cultural backgrounds can help create a stronger neigh-bourhood ecology. In addition, increasing the density in this way enhances the support for public functions: schools, swimming pools, libraries, public transport.

Regent Park was built according to the modernist design principles of the post-war era. Hence in Regent Park and in many similar neighbourhoods, harking back to the nineteenth century was not an option. Its morphology and street layout simply did not allow it. So, should all modernist neighbourhoods follow the example of Regent Park and be demolished before being built back up again? We think not. Overturning these neighbourhoods completely is neither desirable nor feasible. It is costly and its effectiveness in terms of improving people's standard of living questionable.[8] With this caveat in mind, it does not mean there is no room or need for physical interventions. The question is what type of intervention is helpful. People-based and place-based policies are often misleadingly present-ed as mutually exclusive and incompatible adjectives. The former is usually advocated over the latter: the focus should be on 'poor *people*, not poor places'.[9]

[5] Academy of Architecture of Amsterdam University of the Arts, 'Research group Tabula Scripta', 2020. Available at: http://bit.do/fJKnw (accessed 20 February 2020).

[6] D. Snowden, 'The Evolutionary Potential of the Present', *Cognitive Edge*, 29 August 2015. Available at: http://bit.do/fJ4tP (accessed 20 February 2020).

[7] IRP, *The Weight of Cities*, 2018.

[8] E.M. Miltenburg and H.G. van de Werfhorst, 'Finding a Job: The Role of the Neighbourhood for Different Household Configurations over the Life Course', *European Sociological Review* 33, no. 1 (2017), pp. 30–45.

[9] E.L. Glaeser, *The Triumph of the City: How Our Greatest Invention Makes Us Richer, Smarter, Greener, Healthier and Happier* (New York, NY: Penguin, 2011), p. 9 (emphasis in original).

And indeed, attempts to mix deprived neighbourhoods should be approached with some suspicion, as they are 'mainly treating the symptoms of inequalities rather than the causes'.[10] This goes back to what we discussed in the introduction: oftentimes it is not so much the negative *effect* that the neighbourhood has on people, but the fact that the neighbourhood *attracts* certain people.

However, some neighbourhoods lack access to jobs, basic amenities, a safe environment, or a minimal construction quality of homes. You could call it a lack of basic spatial primary goods.[11] In these cases, it is difficult to see how to improve the overall neighbourhood ecology without getting some basic conditions right first. Many of the post-war districts dominated by modernist high-rise struggle with a structure that is ill-suited for interaction and learning. In addition, the structures create the anonymity that fosters crime and unsafety. In such neighbourhoods, some physical intervention may be inevitable. The trick lies in finding ways to keep the best of the modernist structure but add new elements that allow for the development of a supporting neighbourhood ecology. Regent Park and Overvecht show that any physical intervention must be carefully related to the existing social infrastructures.

5. Skin in the Neighbourhood, Ownership for the Public Domain

In the book, we introduced the idea of 'skin in the neighbourhood', referring to the fact that neighbourhoods function better and are more adaptive if key actors have a longer commitment to the place, beyond the initial building or reconstruction phase. A finding of this book is that commitment to the collective domain of a neighbourhood is important. A front door should not open up to the city directly; a good neighbourhood ecology provides an array of 'in-between' functions, from affordable shopping to places to meet, from community centres to amenities like affordable swimming pools and sports grounds. The best neighbourhoods we came across, particularly Vauban, are those where people share some sort of ownership over the public domain. Here it may be helpful to hark back to the threefold categorization that Lyn Lofland made, way back in 1973.[12] Between the 'public' and 'private' space, she argued, cities often have a 'parochial' collective space; this is not entirely public, and not entirely private either, but it allows for safe encounters of a different kind. Think of collectivized public spaces in between housing blocks such as parks, squares, and playgrounds.

Good neighbourhoods characteristically have 'nodes'[13] where the neighbourhood has its shared public space. Part of creating well-functioning neighbourhoods can be a form of 'placemaking' aimed at creating precisely such nodes. But the atmosphere of such places is difficult to create, and very easily

[10] P. Cheshire, 'Policies for Mixed Communities: Faith-based Displacement Activity?', *ESRC Workshop on Gentrification and Social Mix* (London: King's College, 2008), p. 30.

[11] See S. Moroni, *Etica e Territorio: Prospettive di Filosofia Politica per la Pianificazione Territoriale* (Milan: Franco Angeli, 1997). This work is based on John Rawls' notion of social primary goods. See J. Rawls, *A Theory of Justice* (Cambridge, MA: Harvard University Press, 1971).

[12] L.H. Lofland, *A World of Strangers: Order and Action in Urban Public Space* (New York, NY: Basic Books, 1973).

[13] Lynch, *The Image of the City*, 1960.

jeopardized if the 'wrong' shops or services take over. Here, particular legal provisions such as associations, cooperatives, or clubs may enable creating and upkeeping a well-functioning public domain. If real estate for retail is put in an association or cooperative, this can be a way to avoid some of the negative effects of gentrification, as certain functions are driven out because the rents become unaffordable. Such legal provisions would allow to consciously work to maintain certain ecological qualities of the neighbourhood. Nowadays, such legal forms apply predominantly to high-rise condominiums where common spaces are collectively managed in homeowners' associations. We argue this can also be applied 'horizontally', to single-family housing, but also to other forms of (commercial) property and land use. In other words, to any form of 'urban commons' connected to any form of privately-owned space. There is, however, an important challenge in this regard. Property rights are by definition exclusionary; they exist to define the boundaries between the rights and duties of people. Nevertheless, it is possible to design rules of access and rules of conduct that strike a balance between collective management and public (open) access. These rules can also be designed in such a way that *exclusionary* (rights) does not turn into *exclusive* spaces, that is, spaces for affluent users only. In Vauban we came across examples of how affordable housing and retail space can be managed and retained by cooperatives.

6. Creating, Capturing, and Retaining Neighbourhood Value by Scoping

In the essay at the beginning of this book, we made the case for creating value, capturing it, and investing it back into the neighbourhood. To study this we introduced the notion of a neighbourhood value chain. Our cases show examples where either the spatial scope or the temporal scope of development was extended to be able to capture value and invest it, also into goods and services that can only be provided against sub-market prices, such as affordable housing. Portland's Pearl District is an example where the extension of the spatial scope has helped to create and retain value in the area. This neighbourhood has experienced a process of gentrification over the past decades, which was accompanied by a rise in property values. Normally, gentrification makes it difficult or sometimes impossible for low- and middle-income households to settle in such areas. However, in Pearl District 'tax increment financing' (TIF) has been used to tap into these value increases and use them for the provision of affordable housing. Over the years, TIF and other financial sources have helped to construct 2,200 affordable homes in other parts of the District.[14] An example of extending the temporal scope can be found in Oakland's EcoBlock. In EcoBlock, investments are made in renewable energy and wastewater treatment in a block of thirty to forty (semi)detached housing units. One of the reasons why these investments are feasible is that they

[14] J. Cortright, 'A Solution for Displacement: TIF for Affordable Housing', *CityCommentary*, 11 June 2019. Available at: http://bit.do/fJ4tV (accessed 20 February 2020).

are made collectively and therefore economize on scale. Moreover, savings on water and energy costs offset the initial investments. Legal rules enable such forms of temporal and spatial 'scoping'.

7. Gigantic Ambitions, Simple Rules

Decarbonizing our cities is a massive task. Unless deeply contested solutions like negative-emission technologies (such as carbon capture and storage), nuclear energy, or geo-engineering are widely adopted, cities need to start consuming much less energy and make sure the energy they do consume is renewable.[15] These challenges require multiple answers to a simple question: are we ambitious enough in the way we build our neighbourhoods for the future?

The findings of this book are mixed. If we look at the technical or supply side, a lot is already happening, both in terms of climate mitigation and adaptation. Examples are the complete over-hauls in EcoBlock, passive housing in Kronsberg, or climate-adaptive designs in Bo01. However, as we saw in both Bo01 and Regent Park, green buildings can well be inhabited by 'grey' people. A building can have all the possible certificates (BREEAM, LEED, and what have you) but sustainability on paper can never compete with unsustainable lifestyles. In Regent Park we saw that unsustainable behaviour can simply be a result of a lack of awareness of, or unfamiliarity with, technology—mistaking a smart meter for a clock. However, lifestyle discussions can also refer to more fundamental issues. Should we have access to private vehicles the way we are used to? Should our apartments become smaller and should we start sharing kitchens and laundry rooms to increase density and lower the electricity and heating demand? Should what you eat and wear have a limited impact on the planet if you live in a sustainable neighbourhood?

Prescribing behaviour to prevent unsustainable outcomes is often seen as paternalistic and at odds with the principles of our liberal-democratic society. However, our cases show examples where the desired behaviour is not prescribed but facilitated while prohibiting undesired behaviour at the same time. Several neighbourhoods (GWL, Vauban, Merwede) restrict car use while stimulating sustainable alternatives. No parking spots are available, and the public space is inaccessible for motorized traffic. An even more creative approach was found in Bo01. In their green points system, restrictions were combined with stimuli. Developers had to 'score' at least ten green points out of thirty-five. They could choose which ones they wanted; the options ranged from bird boxes to green roofs.

The green points system is an example of the simple rules we discussed in the introduction. They set very clear targets and proscribe undesired behaviour and design outcomes but do not detail the means to get there. Alternatives can and are actively stimulated. If properly regulated, such simple rules could enable creative and ambitious neighbourhood development.

[15] See for instance: D.P. van Vuuren et al., 'Alternative Pathways to the 1.5 C Target Reduce the Need for Negative Emission Technologies', *Nature Climate Change* 8, no. 5 (2018), p. 391–397.

8. Planners are Critical to Success and Come in Different Guises

All the neighbourhoods we looked into had committed 'makers' that drove change based on idealism or conviction. What bound them was their attempt to create cities that are markedly different from the mainstream, and to deliver on the challenge of finding answers to long-term issues of sustainability and inclusion. We cannot do without individuals who think in an integrative way, who can deal with people from many different communities, who can attend to detail without losing sight of the bigger picture, who know about words, numbers, and images. Planners are 'guardians of the long term'. Good planners feel comfortable chatting to residents they meet on a stroll through the neighbourhood. A good planner also knows that people can become emotional about changes that will affect their lives. A good planner knows that conflict is not necessarily bad, that it can be generative.[16] At the same time, a good planner never loses sight of the long term. A good planner always keeps in mind that natural gas for heating and cooking is not viable in the long run, no matter how fond residents might be of their stove. A good planner looks beyond the four-year electoral cycle, when an alderman or mayor might be gone but the neighbourhood is still there. A good planner resists the urge to always respond to the pressing issues of the short run, something which John Dewey referred to as the 'tendencies needing constant regulation'.[17]

This is far from an easy job, and the findings on the extent to which the planners' craftsmanship worked out in our three case studies are, again, mixed. The role of the planner can be fulfilled by different actors. It can be the sensitive neighbourhood professionals like Keir Brownstone, who is acting as an energy manager in a housing corporation in Regent Park, or Marina Slijkerman in Overvecht, who sees great potential in the neighbourhood and allocates subsidies to residents' initiatives she deems empowering. It can be a developer who strives to go beyond a mere bricks-and-mortar perspective. Such as Mitchell Cohen from Daniels Corporation, who went out on a limb in Regent Park and pledged to frontload the construction of a new community park, or the developer Heijmans, where Peter van der Gugten is not just after making places but also operating them for the greater good of the neighbourhood. And then there are local politicians, such as Ilmar Reepalu in Malmö, who acknowledge the crises that their cities or neighbourhoods are struggling with, and who spark the debate about how to break out of the downward spiral and open up to a radical, new imaginary.

[16] N. Verloo, *Negotiating Urban Conflict: Conflicts as Opportunity for Urban Democracy* (Amsterdam: University of Amsterdam, 2015).

[17] J. Dewey, *How We Think* (Boston, MA: D.C. Heath and Company, 1910).

[18] J. Throgmorton, *Planning as Persuasive Storytelling* (Chicago, IL: University of Chicago Press, 1996).

9. Shared Storylines Help, but Require Effort

James Throgmorton famously wrote that 'planning is persuasive storytelling about the future'.[18] Our cases, once again, show how important storytelling is.

Both in Bo01 and Regent Park a broad coalition of actors shared a storyline, in which past, present, and future were combined into one shared narrative. In such cases, a storyline essentially coordinates: people know how to go on, appreciate the qualities they are looking for, show they are aware of the efforts that went into making the neighbourhood a better place, and know what to do within the domains of their respective organizations.

It is something that keeps coming back: discourses organize coalitions of stakeholders. However, what our research also brought out is how much effort goes into mutual exchanges *before* such a joint storyline emerges and true 'discourse coalitions' shape up. The best storylines emerge out of a process of interaction. Indeed, often the emergence of such a storyline becomes itself part of the storyline ('At one moment we realized that…'). It seems that much more attention is needed to understand how you arrive at generative storylines. In Overvecht we saw how difficult it is to come to a shared storyline. While there is a plethora of initiatives, a narrative that 'glues' them together is lacking, thus preventing the desired social-ecological renovation taking off. In Regent Park we saw planners who actively took this on, speaking to many stakeholders, listening to stories, trying out elements of possible planning interventions, testing the waters. We call this approach 'stringing beads', referring to the way in which, one by one, one wins actors over to a particular future. Apart from this individual 'planning as diplomacy' we know from other cases that collective gatherings are always crucial. Yet when these meetings are taken on in too managerial a way, they are not likely to produce the desired results. We insist on the importance of dramaturgy in this regard. Nothing as valuable for creating shared storylines as the joint experience of finding one. Moreover, joint futuring takes time. If not done right, people think that first proposals are 'plans' that will be executed; if done in a more sophisticated way, people will realize that they too have a role to play, that their concerns are acknowledged, that their contributions are appreciated. Regent Park is interesting in this regard as it showed a planning process in which requests (such as for a cricket ground) were included in the plan, and where a diverse community found ways to discuss the neighbourhoods they wanted, based on the awareness that their contribution was taken seriously. We noticed that this open planning process itself had become an element of the story that many participants shared of Regent Park.

Outlook

The idea of the neighbourhood as a *Leitbild* or imaginary may be modest in intent, it is desperately needed at the same time. All over the world, urban density is going down, not up as a sustainable urban future would require. Countries like Canada and the United States struggle to get a basic public transport system going, which is crucial if we want to reduce car dependency. India builds a hundred new smart cities, but basically following a modernist logic, as do fast urbanizing countries like Turkey. Here the idea of building strong neighbourhoods is not on the table. China built many of its new cities in modernist high-rise format, at long distances from work, and exports this typology to Africa but only recently seems to turn to building cities with strong neighbourhoods. So, while we work from a selected set of neighbourhoods in the Global North, we still think that this exercise is of broader importance for the debate about global urbanization. The good news is that we see new developments, such as in the eastern extension of the Ethiopian capital of Addis Abeba, where an attempt is made to create neighbourhoods and where alternatives for automobility (a light rail) are structuring the new layout of the rapidly growing city.

Overall, we hope to have conveyed that well-functioning neighbourhoods are ultimately liveable. We would like to take issue with any suggestion that fighting climate change leads to a catastrophic loss of quality of life. If we were to create new inclusive neighbourhoods for the future, we can look forward to new sustainable ways of living which will, most likely, have many extra merits, including wasting less time in commutes and more social interaction. A world of neighbourhoods offers an attractive idea of a sustainable future.

Appendix

Authors

Edwin Buitelaar (*1979) is a professor in Land and Real Estate Development at Utrecht University, senior researcher at the PBL Netherlands Environmental Assessment Agency, and research fellow at the Amsterdam School of Real Estate. His work focuses on the coming about of urban development, with a particular focus on housing, commercial real estate, planning law, land policy, land-use planning, and the financial side of development. Recent publications include: *Planning, Law and Economics* (with Barrie Needham and Thomas Hartmann) (2018) and *Cities, Economic Inequality and Justice* (with Anet Weterings and Roderik Ponds) (2017).

Chris ten Dam (*1996) is a graduate student in Energy Science. She focuses on the use of energy for heating and transport in the built environment. She obtained her bachelor's degree (summa cum laude) at Amsterdam University College and worked as a research assistant at Utrecht University's Urban Futures Studio from 2017 to 2019, where she assisted in preparing 'Places of Hope' (Leeuwarden/Fryslân Cultural Capital of Europe, 2018).

Maarten Hajer (*1962) studied Political Science and Urban and Regional Planning at the University of Amsterdam and received his PhD in Politics from the University of Oxford. He is a distinguished professor of Urban Futures and scientific director of the university-wide strategic theme 'Pathways to Sustainability' at Utrecht University. Hajer holds an extraordinary professorship at Stellenbosch University and is a member of the United Nations' International Resource Panel (IRP). Recent exhibitions include: 'Places of Hope', Leeuwarden/Fryslân Cultural Capital of Europe, 2018; International Architecture Biennale Rotterdam, 2016. Publications include: *Smart about Cities: Visualizing the Challenge of 21st Century Urbanism* (2014); *Authoritative Governance* (2009); *In Search of New Public Domain* (2001); *The Politics of Environmental Discourse* (1995).

Martijn van den Hurk (*1987) is an assistant professor in the Department of Human Geography and Spatial Planning, and a fellow of the Urban Futures Studio in the Faculty of Geosciences at Utrecht University. He studied Spatial Planning and Public Administration at Radboud University Nijmegen and obtained his PhD in Political Science at the University of Antwerp. His scholarship is aimed at understanding the institutional arrangements that underlie transformations in urban infrastructures and city building. Van den Hurk has published academically in the fields of planning and public administration, particularly on public-private partnerships, contracts, and urban regeneration.

Peter Pelzer (*1986) is an assistant professor in Spatial Planning and Urban Futures in the Department of Human Geography and Spatial Planning, and a fellow of the Urban Futures Studio in the Faculty of Geosciences at Utrecht University. He curated the 'Post-Fossil City Contest' (Utrecht, 2017) and is a core instructor in the mixed-classroom module titled 'Techniques of Futuring'. Pelzer has published in both academic and popular media on imagination, urban mobility, and the science-policy interface. He draws a lot of inspiration from teaching the future generation of planners.

Acknowledgements

We would like to extend our sincere gratitude to all those who have devoted their valuable time to help us research this book. Thanks to all who contributed pieces of information, provided research assistance, or gave feedback. While it is impossible to mention everybody, here are those who helped us the most.

First, our deep and sincere gratitude goes to our interview respondents. To Martine August, Keir Brownstone, Sarah Craig, Will Fleissig, John Gladki, Ken Greenberg, Melanie Hare, Sureya Ibrahim, Jed Kilbourn, Emma Loewen, and Amanda Santo in Canada. To Mikael Edelstam, Trevor Graham, Roger Hildingsson, Annika Kruuse, Christer Larsson, Per-Arne Nilsson, Joakim Nordqvist, Mattias Örtenvik, Per Rosén, Cord Siegel, Joseph Strahl, and Johannes Stripple in Sweden. To Alwin Beernink, Dick Boeve, Leon Borlée, Thijs van Dieren, Mark Elbers, Peter van der Gugten, Gerbert Hengelaar, Sebastiaan van der Hijden, Peter Hulshof, Michiel Jongmans, Fred Jonker, Marianne Lamberts, Marianne Nevens, Valentijn Nouwens, Arjen van Ree, Marina Slijkerman, Reijnder Jan Spits, Bastiaan Staffhorst, Ad Tourné, Els Wegdam, and Sander Willemsen in the Netherlands. You are all busy working in or on neighbourhoods and provided us with the insights without which a book like this would be inconceivable.

A special acknowledgement to the people who helped us build the database for this book by generously providing information for the vignettes: Carsten Arlund, Hannu Asikainen, Anne-Perrine Avrin, Anni Bäckman, Sara Bartolomeo, Katharina Bayer, Luca Bertolini, Niels Bethlowsky Kristensen, Lene Bjerg Kristensen, Norm Bourassa, Rich Brown, Emmelie Brownlee, Maria Büchner, Tara Connor, Eden Dabbs, Andreas Delleske, Pooran Desai, Troy Doss, Julie Gustafson, Ute Heda, Josh Hillburt, Andreas Hofer, Marcel Janssen, Hanna Joos, Daniel Kammen, Anthony Kittel, Eva Klamméus, Lykke Leonardsen, Anthony Nahas, Maika Nicholson, Katharina Pfaff, Diego Pos, Sandy Robertson, Philipp Späth, Kaisa Spilling, Christine Thomson, Robert Voggesberger, Jonny Wilkinson, and Jill Wullems.

Great appreciation to Isabel Liedtke, Esli Severijn, and the teams of BRIGHT/The Cloud Collective—Gerjan Streng, Thijs van Spaandonk, Stephanie Ete, and Juliette van Baar—and MUST Stedebouw—Sebastian van Berkel and Tea Hazizulfi—with whom we collaborated on the catalogue and the exhibition for 'Places of Hope'.

To Lisette van Beek, Like Bijlsma, Irene Bronsvoort, Arjan Harbers, Jesse Hoffman, Martine de Jong, Emily Miltenburg, Jeroen Oomen, Suzanne Potjer, Rianne Riemens, Hilde Segond von Banchet, Niels Sorel, Vanessa Timmer, Justus Uitermark, Wytske Versteeg, and Beate Volker, all for their constructive comments on early drafts of the texts we wrote, on the data we collected, and on the images that we sought to use.

This book is the result of transdisciplinary collaboration. We thank the Dutch Ministry of Infrastructure and Water Management (IenW), which provided the initial funding for the research capacity of the Urban Futures Studio devoted to this project, and the Dutch Ministry of the Interior and Kingdom Relations (BZK), which financially supported the research done for the 'Places of Hope' exhibition and the production of this book. Thanks in particular to

Lilian van den Aarsen, Robert Dijksterhuis, Elize de Kock, Hanna Lára Pálsdóttir, Marleen de Ruiter, and Hans Tijl.

We thank the Faculty of Geosciences of Utrecht University for the freedom they granted us to explore new ways of bringing together academics from different disciplinary backgrounds (urban planning, futuring, governance, and energy sciences) with policymakers to create exhibitions and text that are societally relevant and accessible, and that meet academic standards at the same time. While initiated by the Urban Futures Studio, the book is the result of a truly collaborative effort of three institutes within Utrecht University: the Urban Futures Studio, the Department of Human Geography and Spatial Planning, and the research hub Transforming Infrastructures for Sustainable Cities, part of the strategic theme Pathways to Sustainability of Utrecht University.

Index

Image Credits

Appendix

Colophon

Authors Maarten Hajer, Peter Pelzer,
Martijn van den Hurk, Chris ten Dam,
Edwin Buitelaar

Copy-editing Leo Reijnen

Proofreading Els Brinkman

Index Elke Stevens

Maps Till Hormann

Image research Line Arngaard

Graphic design Catalogtree, catalogtree.net

Typefaces LL Circular Std by Laurenz Brunner

Paper inside Amber Graphic 120 gr.

Paper cover Amber Graphic 240 gr.

Lithography KOLORworkx

Printing and binding Wilco, Meppel / Amersfoort (NL)

Partner Urban Futures Studio, Utrecht University

Publisher Pia Pol, Simon Franke & Astrid Vorstermans
— trancity*valiz, Amsterdam (NL)

trancity*valiz  Utrecht University

International distribution

BE/NL/LU: Centraal Boekhuis,
www.centraal.boekhuis.nl

GB/IE: Anagram Books, www.anagrambooks.com

Europe/Asia: Idea Books, www.ideabooks.nl

USA: D.A.P., www.artbook.com

Individual orders: www.valiz.nl; info@valiz.nl

ISBN 978-94-92095-78-7
Printed and bound in the EU

This project was made possible by funding from
the Dutch Ministry of the Interior and Kingdom
Relations (BZK) as well as the Dutch Ministry of
Infrastructure and Water Management (IenW).

 Ministry of the Interior and
Kingdom Relations

 Ministry of Infrastructure
and Water Management